THE SAINSBURY LABORATORY

THE SAINSBURY LABORATORY

Science, Architecture, Art

Stephen Day, John Parker, Steve Rose

black dog
publishing
london uk

CONTENTS

FOREWORD
David Sainsbury
Baron Sainsbury of Turville, Hon FRS

I would like to take the credit for devising the research strategy for the new Sainsbury Laboratory in Cambridge, and for designing the beautiful building in which the laboratory is now housed, but I can only claim credit for backing the three individuals who are responsible for bringing about these two exciting developments.

The first of these three individuals is Roger Freedman, a life-long friend who I first met when we were both undergraduates at King's College, Cambridge. He had already persuaded me in the mid-1980s to fund the highly successful Sainsbury Laboratory for plant molecular pathology in Norwich, and in the 1990s to fund the equally successful Sainsbury Laboratory for computational neuroscience at UCL in London. It was, therefore, an easy decision to make when he came to me with the exciting idea of building a laboratory in Cambridge to understand plant development, using the power of DNA analysis, genetics, advanced microscopy and computation.

I am convinced that not only will plant development be an exciting area of science in the next 25 years, but also one which in time brings important environmental benefits, as well as helping the world meet the challenge of feeding nine billion people in 2050. Roger not only identified the research strategy for the new laboratory, but also, as always, nursed the project through its early stages.

The second person who has played a significant role in this project is my wife, Susie. Roger and I had agreed that the building of the laboratory was not a time to indulge my love of modern architecture. The building should be a utilitarian structure, and we should accept the fact that it would probably be pulled down in 20 years when its facilities would be out of date. Susie, however, pointed out that not to build a beautiful building in the Cambridge Botanic Garden would be a missed opportunity, that it is not necessary to have cost over-runs or delays when producing great architecture, and that a well-designed building can greatly improve the productivity of those who work in it. Fortunately, I accepted her advice. She also played a major role in choosing Stanton Williams as the architects, and had the brilliant idea of funding Norman Ackroyd to go to the Galapagos Islands to get inspiration for the outstanding panels he has done for the building.

The third person who must take great credit for this project is, of course, Alan Stanton, who led the architectural team. When Stanton Williams were

appointed as the architects for the project they were given three basic design criteria for the laboratory by Roger Freedman. These were the best possible use of natural light, the fostering of a sense of community and conviviality, and enough flexibility to accommodate as-yet-unforeseen changes in the nature of plant science.

What is remarkable about the building that Alan and his team have created is that it triumphantly meets all these criteria, as well as being a beautiful building. They have also designed what is in fact a large building in such a way that it fits elegantly into the Botanic Garden, and one that meticulously meets the needs of the scientists who will work in it. I am convinced that in the years ahead it will be seen, in the UK and abroad, as a building which sets a new standard for the design of laboratories.

Finally, I would like to thank Alison Richard, until recently Vice-Chancellor of Cambridge, whose enthusiastic support of the project greatly aided its progress, Peter Hesketh, the Director of the Gatsby Foundation, who managed the project on my behalf, and Stuart Johnson, the Strategic Project Manager, who brought it in on time and budget.

The aim of the project is, of course, to make exciting discoveries. If that happens the credit will rightly go to the scientists, but some part of the credit should also go to the team of people who devised the research strategy for the laboratory and built a beautiful building in which to house it.

David Sainsbury received a BA in 1963 from the University of Cambridge, in 1971 an MBA from Columbia University and an Hon FREng (Hon FEng, in 1994). He was made an Honorary Fellow of the Academy of Medical Sciences and an Honorary Fellow of the Royal Society in 2008. David Sainsbury was raised to the peerage as Baron Sainsbury of Turville, of Turville in the County of Buckinghamshire, 1997. He was awarded the Andrew Carnegie Medal of Philanthropy in 2003.

First page
View from the Limestone Rock Garden across the Lake to a Dawn Redwood (*Metasequoia glyptostroboides*).

Title page
Olive trees in the central court.

Half title page
The facade of The Sainsbury Laboratory.

Page pior to contents page
Terrace of the public cafe.

Contents page
Olive trees in the central court.

Above
View of The Sainsbury Laboratory entrance court.

Overleaf
The Laboratory building and the terrace of the public cafe; the Scented Garden, with wallflowers, alliums and *Wisteria*.

INTRODUCTION

The Sainsbury Laboratory at the University of Cambridge eloquently makes powerful statements about plant science. The most obvious is that plant science is an urgent priority, addressing some of the major challenges of the twenty-first century, such as sustainable secure food and fuel supply.

Perhaps less obvious is the importance of the integration of science, art and nature, with cutting edge science pursued in an architecturally stunning building, surrounded by beautiful art and the Botanic Garden. The perception of science as a cold, soulless, inhuman activity is a major barrier to the adoption of science-based solutions. It is also profoundly misguided. The focus of the lab is to understand, with predictive accuracy, how plants literally conjure themselves out of thin air. Powered by sunlight, plants combine water, carbon dioxide and a sprinkling of salt to build, molecule by molecule, the many and diverse plant forms that surround us. This is an amazing and wonderful thing, and is made all the more so as we begin to understand how it works. The more we know, the more astonishingly beautiful it becomes.

To make progress in understanding the intricate complexities of life takes creativity, ingenuity, intuition and inspiration. The Sainsbury Laboratory provides a fertile ground to realise our ambitious scientific vision, and simultaneously a spectacular public statement about the seamless connection between nature, art and science.

PROFESSOR OTTOLINE LEYSER
Professor of Plant Development and Associate Director,
The Sainsbury Laboratory

When Stanton Williams were chosen to design the new building, the Gatsby Foundation and the University of Cambridge stipulated that they were hoping for a world class building to house a new scientific research institution that would be at the forefront of plant research and attract the best scientists from around the world.

The brief we were given was for a 11,000 square metre plant research centre, that would bring together world-leading scientists in a working environment of the highest quality. The building, in the setting of the lawns of the University's Botanic Garden, had to reconcile complex scientific requirements with the need for a piece of architecture that would also respond to its landscape setting. It should provide a stimulating environment for innovative research and collaboration, containing research laboratories and their associated support areas. It would also contain the University's

The Laboratory seen across the lawn of Cory Lodge.

Herbarium, meeting rooms, an auditorium, social spaces and a new public cafe. An integral feature of the project would also be specially commissioned artworks responding to the science, the setting and the architecture.

The Cambridge University Botanic Garden was conceived in 1831 by Charles Darwin's guide and mentor, John Henslow, as a working research tool in which the diversity of plant species would be systematically ordered and catalogued. The new Sainsbury Laboratory would develop Henslow's agenda, seeking to advance understanding of how this diversity comes about. Its design would therefore be shaped by its integral relationship with the garden beyond.

Professor John Parker, as Director of the Botanic Garden, played an integral part in the development of the design of the building and its relationship to the Garden. As he says later in this book "... the opening of The Sainsbury Laboratory will transform our understanding of plant development, using the power of DNA analysis, genetics and computation. Remarkably, plant development looks back to the Garden's founder, John Henslow. His concerns about diversity, development and the nature of species grew from his background in mathematical and physical science, and were embedded in his experimental approach to biology. The possibility for resolution of his remarkable vision has had to wait nearly 200 years, for the opening of The Sainsbury Laboratory, University of Cambridge, in his beautiful Botanic Garden."

As we considered the building in terms of its landscape setting, we decided to link the internal areas by a continuous route which recalls Charles Darwin's 'thinking path', a way to reconcile nature and thought through the activity of walking. Here the 'thinking path' would function as a space for reflection and debate. Our intention was to promote encounters and interaction between the scientists working in the building, and between them and the landscape.

As we developed the concept, it became apparent that we needed three clear elements to the design:

The building's identity is established externally by the way in which it is expressed and experienced as a series of interlinked yet distinct volumes of differing height grouped around three sides of a central courtyard, the fourth side of which is made up of trees planted by Henslow in the nineteenth century. The internal circulation and communal areas focus upon this central court, opening into it at ground level and onto a raised terrace above in order to provide immediate physical connections between the laboratory and its surroundings.

The second key element was that all the working areas—laboratories, offices, etc.—were incorporated onto a single floor to encourage communication and improve relationships between functional areas. Set at first floor level, it would allow the use of natural overhead light—a first for a laboratory and a feature that would improve the working environment as well as being energy efficient. Further visual connections are created by the careful use of glazing

A scientist at work in the Laboratory, testing plant specimens.

in the building. Windows provide views of the courtyard and the garden beyond, allowing these internal areas to be read as integral elements of the outdoor landscape.

The third element responding to the challenges in the brief was to create a layout to encourage scientists to meet and dialogue at an informal level— the chance conversation and the 'corridor meeting' should be encouraged. Thus the building would have an internal 'street' around the courtyard with sitting areas and an all important coffee machine to encourage that dialogue and the 'accidental' conversations that could lead to scientific discovery.

The architecture of the new laboratory building reinterprets the tradition of the Greek stoa, the monastic cloister and the collegiate court, all of which were intended, to some extent, for contemplation and meetings. As a result, past, present and future are connected. The design has produced a building that is rooted in its setting. There are two storeys visible above ground and a further subterranean level so that the overall effect is strongly horizontal as a result. Solidity is implied by the use of bands of limestone and exposed concrete, recalling geological strata and, indeed, the Darwinian idea of evolution over time, as well as the permanence which one might expect of a major research centre.

ALAN STANTON
Stanton Williams

Above
The public cafe terrace with Norman Ackroyd's *Galapagos*.

Opposite
View from the terrace above the public cafe into the central court of the Laboratory building.

In the Foreword to this book David, my husband, describes the evolution of the ideas behind the design of The Sainsbury Laboratory, and he and Roger Freedman set a concise but challenging brief for the architects who would be selected to design this new centre for cutting-edge plant science. My role was to help ensure that the architectural practice who won the competition would be responsive to the scope, the science, and the ambitions and hopes of the clients. The architects' approach to the design of the laboratory had to be sensitive to the extraordinary setting, and also had to respond to the specific and complex needs of the scientists who would work there.

Alan Stanton, Paul Williams and the team at Stanton Williams have conceived and designed a building which answers all the demands of the challenges set, meets the technical demands of the science, and uses natural light, subtle lines, and generous proportions to deliver a world-class building. Unusually, in the often fractious world of design and construction, this exciting project has been completed entirely harmoniously, on time and on budget, and the experience of the client and construction teams, and their advisors, has been stimulating, rewarding and amicable.

The Sainsbury Laboratory sets a new paradigm for the design of a centre for scientific research. Its adaptable, tranquil and enviable working environment is lifted to another level through a series of interlinked spaces, each beautiful in its own right.

Susie Sainsbury
—June 2011

A grouping of Beech (*Fagus*) trees in the Botanic Garden.

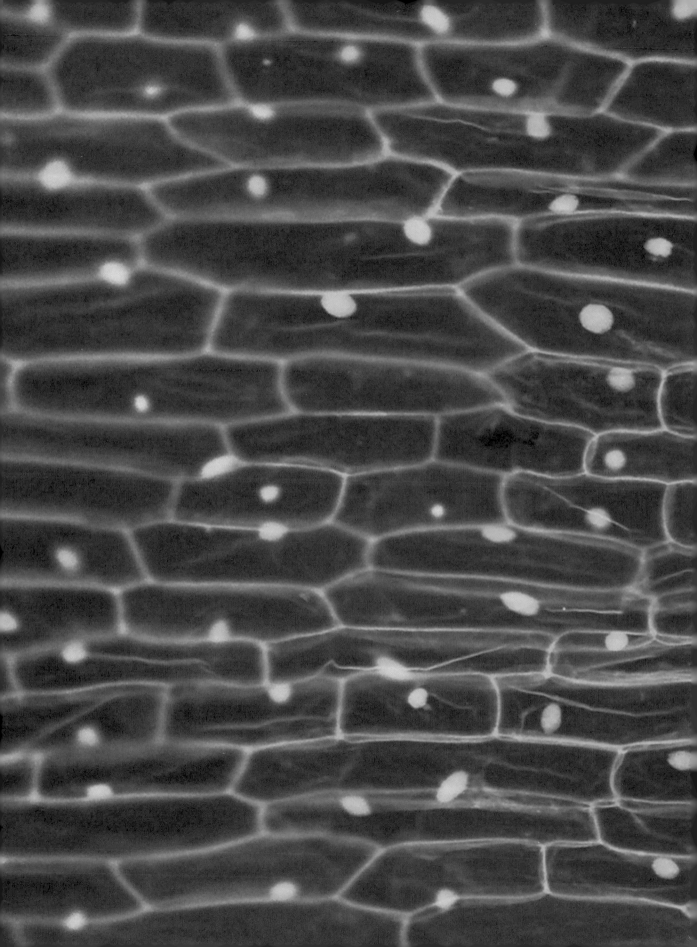

UNDERSTANDING
PLANT DEVELOPMENT
Stephen Day

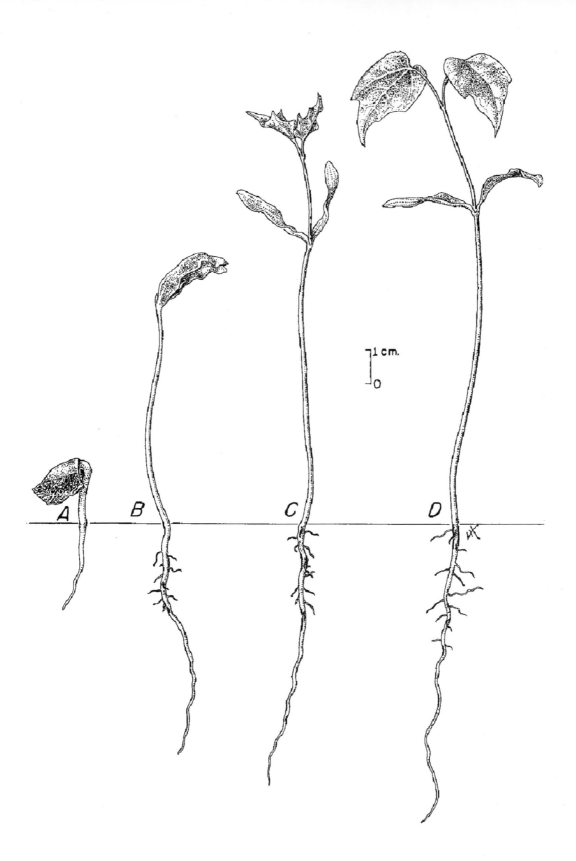

WHEN THE LAND TURNED GREEN

Four hundred and fifty million years ago, Earth's oceans teemed with life but her continents were almost bare. Mountains of naked rock rose from plains of sands and gravels that were scoured by floods and unstable, rapidly-shifting rivers. Most of the land was home to little more than micro-organisms and, possibly, lichens. However, along the water's edge, the first land plants were appearing and an eons long transformation of the landscape was beginning. As they spread into ever wider regions, plants helped capture and build up soils, easing the severity of floods by allowing the land to soak up water, and stabilising river courses by sending their roots into the river banks. The new breeds of plants also, of course, supplied the food and habitats that the animal kingdom needed to follow them ashore.

All of this depended, and depends, on plant development—the process by which plants establish and elaborate their forms. The competition to survive and reproduce on land drove plants to evolve specialised structures, such as roots to collect water and nutrients, and stems and leaves to compete for light. So whereas plant life in the oceans is still almost entirely restricted to seaweeds and microscopic algae, land plants have evolved into today's vast diversity of species, from tiny mosses to an estimated one hundred thousand different types of tree. In studying plant development, therefore, researchers are attempting to understand not only how the intricate structures that make up each plant arise, but also how the many different forms of plant life evolved and how individual plants are able to adapt their growth to their particular habitats.

BUILT BY CELLS

> … our Microscope informs us that the substance of Cork is altogether fill'd with Air, and that that Air is perfectly enclosed in little Boxes or Cells distinct from one another.
> ROBERT HOOKE, 1665

When Hooke placed a slice of cork (the bark of the cork oak) beneath his microscope, what he saw were dead walls that had once surrounded living plant cells. His description began a transformation in the study of biology. Every slice of every organism that scientists placed beneath a lens revealed itself to be composed either of cells or of structures made by cells. There was one, inescapable conclusion—cells were the architects of the living world. Ever since this realisation, researchers who have wanted to understand plant or animal development have had a single, central question: How do the individual cells that make up a plant or animal organise themselves to construct a functional organism?

Opposite
A diagram showing the development of a flowering plant (maple) seedling.

Above
Male haircap moss (*Polytrichum* sp.) in Sneads Ferry, North Carolina.

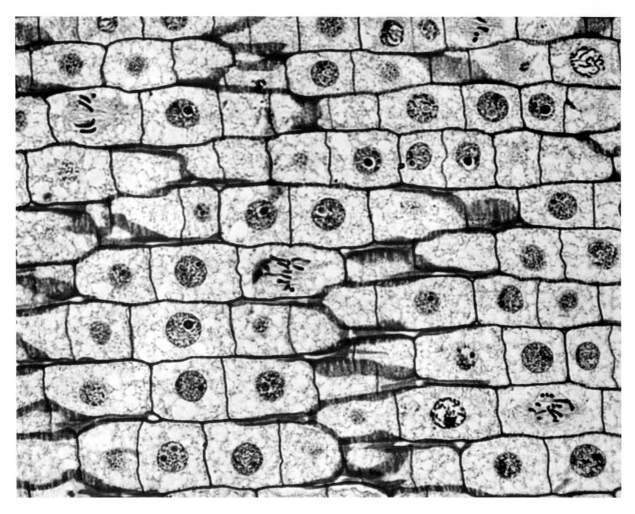

Above
Photomicrograph showing cell divisions in onion (*Allium*). This is a 'panorama' of four photographs originally taken at a magnification of X40.

Opposite top
Photomicrograph of an embryo taken from an *Arabidopsis thaliana* seed. The photograph shows a section through the shoot tip of the embryo. The ball of cells in the centre is the apical meristem, which becomes the growing point of a seedling shoot after germination. The apical meristem lies between the bases of the two cotyledons (seed leaves) from which vascular tissue can be seen entering the embryo's stem (the hypocotyl).

Opposite bottom
A composite photomicrograph of an early *Arabidopsis thaliana* embryo. The embryo is shown in red (the purple tissue is part of the seed) and at this stage consists of a ball of just eight cells. It is connected to maternal tissue by a strand of cells called the "suspensor", also shown in red. The uppermost cell of the suspensor eventually contributes to the development of the embryonic root tip.

After centuries of microscopy, we now have good, descriptive answers. For example, most research on plant development has focused on flowering plants (a huge group that includes the broad-leafed trees, the grasses, all major food crops, and, of course, every species whose showy relatives find their way into the herbaceous border or florist). Scientists have found that despite their diversity, all flowering plants employ very similar underlying patterns of development.

Flowering plants begin life as a fertilised egg cell inside a parent flower. The fertilised egg develops into an embryo—a plant in miniature consisting of a rudimentary shoot and root—lying inside a seed. When the seed germinates, the embryo elongates, breaking free of the seedcase and sending the root down into the soil and the shoot up into the air. From then on, the plant's development centres around the tips of its shoots and roots, specifically around regions called "meristems" in which cell divisions initiate new tissues and organs. The shoot meristem, for example, is a dome of cells at the very centre of the shoot tip. As they divide, cells in the meristem initiate the growth of each new leaf and each new section of stem.

Development continues in a repeating pattern throughout the flowering plant's life. Seedlings typically begin with just two active meristems—a shoot meristem at the top and a root meristem at the bottom—but during their

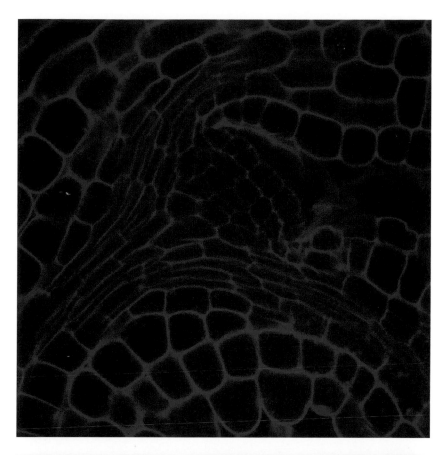

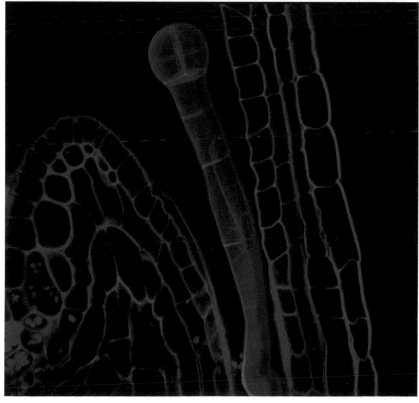

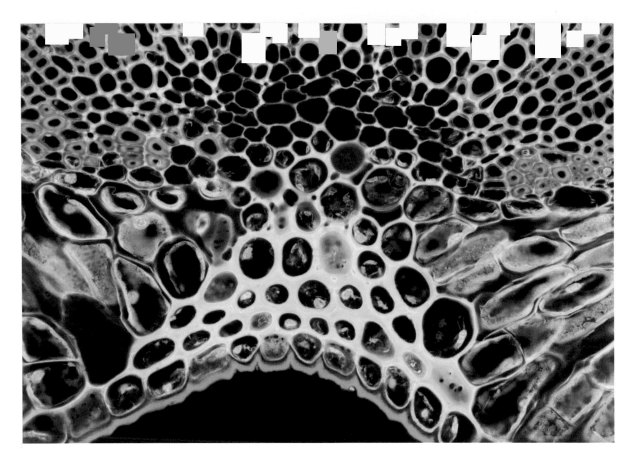

growth, they produce many more. New shoot meristems form at the base of each leaf, while new root meristems arise behind the growing root tip from cells within the root. Each new meristem can then build a new shoot or root branch complete with its own new meristems. Meristems can also change how they behave, such as switching from producing a leafy shoot to making a flower.

The challenge now is to go beyond a simple description and discover the mechanisms that control plant development. Consider the growth of a new leaf. For a leaf to 'work', each cell has to act appropriately for its position. So on the upper leaf surface, cells might choose between making a protective hair and becoming a flat, waterproofing 'pavement' cell. Inside the leaf, some cells must become part of the leaf veins, while others specialise for photosynthesis. Studying leaf development, researchers have discovered that leaf cells coordinate their behaviour through intricate exchanges of signalling molecules, including signals that pass between cells to let each cell 'know' how to behave for its particular position.

Leaf cells also make group decisions about the leaf as a whole. For example, cells in a young leaf detect the hormone 'auxin' (familiar to gardeners as the active ingredient of rooting powder) and respond by growing larger more quickly. As a result, tobacco plants genetically modified to produce extra copies of an auxin receptor have leaves in which cells grow up to twice their normal volume. But these leaves are still the normal size and shape. Somehow the leaf cells are able to respond to the leaf's absolute size and collectively compensate for their own increased dimensions

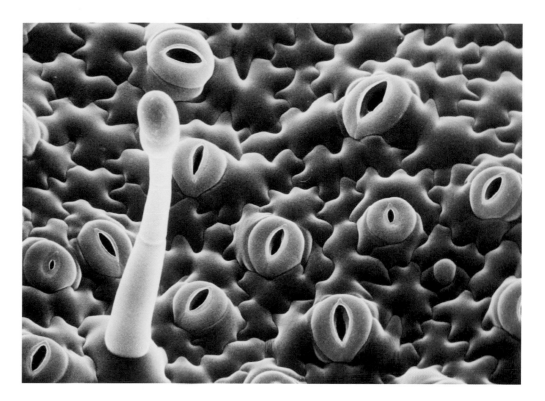

by dividing less often, producing a leaf of the normal size but consisting of fewer, larger cells.

At a still higher level of complexity, each new leaf responds to signals sent by other parts of the plant. Hence holly leaves are most spiky on the lower branches of the tree, where they are in reach of browsing animals. To achieve this, the cells forming a new holly leaf must receive and respond to information about that leaf's overall position—it is thought that this may involve a signal indicating how close the leaf is to the plant's roots. Furthermore, holly leaves are spikier if they are growing on a branch that has previously been browsed, showing that cells in new leaves can modify how they build a leaf according to signals telling them about their branch's history. Lastly, leaf growth responds to information from the plant's environment. For example, plants' ability to track the seasons of the year lets them determine when leaves form; plants' perceptions of the amount of light, water and nutrients they receive regulate the size of leaves; and plants' responses to both gravity and the time of day control the angle of leaves.

That the collective result of all these influences on cell behaviour is a functioning plant rather than chaos is largely thanks to built-in feedback. Unlike information in a perfectly drawn-up architectural plan, which could flow in a single direction (from blueprint, to builders, to building), researchers have found that the information that controls plant development flows in cycles—allowing each decision to affect subsequent decisions. For example, auxin produced by new leaves is transported down to the roots where it induces certain cells to initiate new roots. Roots produce the hormone 'cytokinin' which is carried up to the shoot and promotes new shoot branches. The cycle is part of the mechanism that balances growth above the ground with that below.

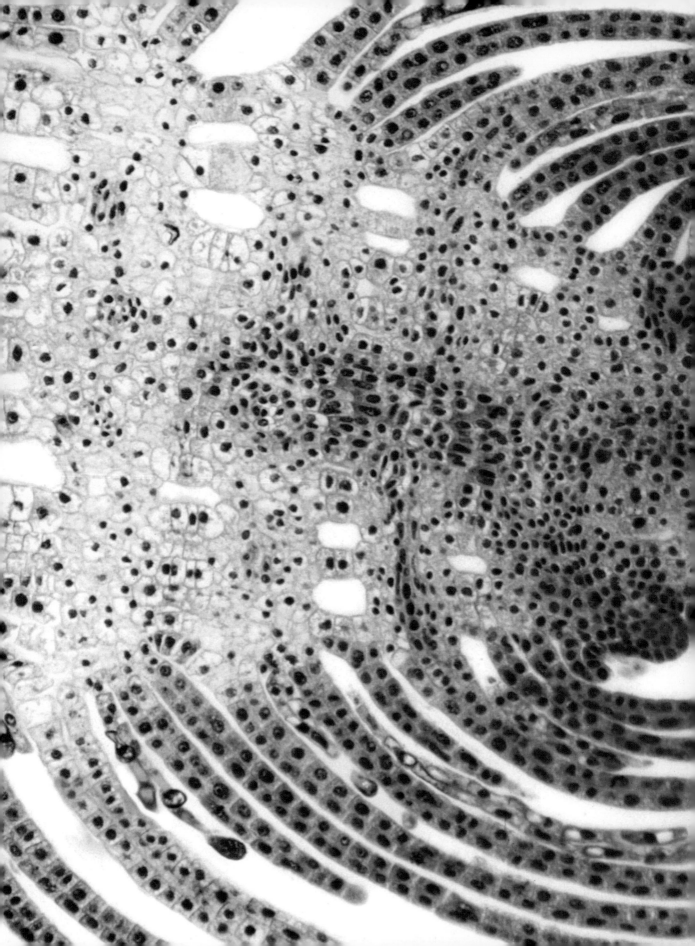

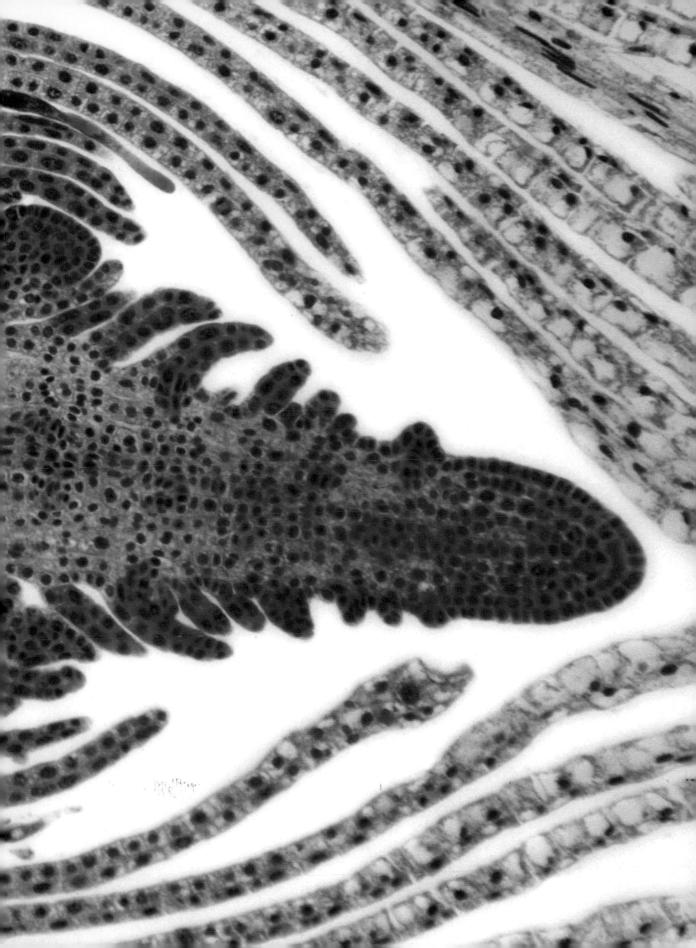

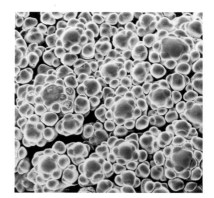

MAKING THE PARTS

To understand how each part of a plant—a leaf, a root, a flower, etc.—constructs itself, researchers are going to have to untangle the complex web of molecular signals that controls the process and explain how these signals ensure that each cell plays its proper role. Fortunately, they have a central principle to guide their investigations: biologists have discovered that to a large extent, the behaviour of each cell is controlled by a relatively small number of 'master' genes.

This realisation came from research into genetic mutations that derail normal patterns of growth. For example, some mutations can rearrange parts of the plant, such as making stamens appear in the place of petals in a flower, or changing whole flowers to resemble leafy shoots. Other mutations 'delete' parts, for instance resulting in seedlings that germinate without a shoot meristem (the growing tip of the shoot, see above).

Investigating the genes affected by such mutations shows that very often they encode proteins that bind to DNA to control whether other genes are switched 'on' or 'off'. In other words, they are master genes whose function is to control overall gene activity in the cell. The combination of active master genes varies in different parts of the plant, controlling patterns of gene activity so that each part develops correctly. When a master gene is mutated, some of the combinations change and so parts of the plant are rearranged or deleted. Because of their dramatic effects, mutations affecting such genes are by no means confined to the laboratory. For example, they are the cause of the excessive petal production by showy 'double-flowered' garden plants. Similarly, the white heart of a cauliflower arises because the plant carries a mutation in a master gene needed to develop flowers. The cauliflower heart grows as the plant attempts to produce flowers and, rather obviously, fails. (In this case, the block isn't complete and some flowers eventually form—hence cauliflower seeds are available for the next year.)

The central role of master genes has naturally led researchers to investigate how such genes are themselves controlled. In particular, plant biologists are attempting to unpick how the activities of master genes are tied to the web of signals passing between cells during plant growth. For example, some of the master genes that help direct cells to form a root are activated in response to high concentrations of the plant hormone auxin. Such high concentrations occur at the root-end of the embryo forming inside a seed. They also form at the base of cut shoots, helping to explain why cuttings make new roots and why the auxin in rooting powder is effective. Another vital question is how the correct combinations of active master genes are maintained as each part of the plant forms: what stops a petal from turning into a stamen, or a shoot from

Above
False colour electron micrograph of the head of a cauliflower. Each bulge is the apical meristem of an individual inflorescence (flowering stem). Normally, the inflorescence apical meristem produces flowers. However, cauliflowers carry a mutation that prevents this, meaning that, instead, each apical meristem produces more apical meristems. The process repeats itself, forming the white mass that is the cauliflower head.

Opposite
Buttercup (*Ranunculus japonicus*) root with a newly formed lateral root emerging from it (top).

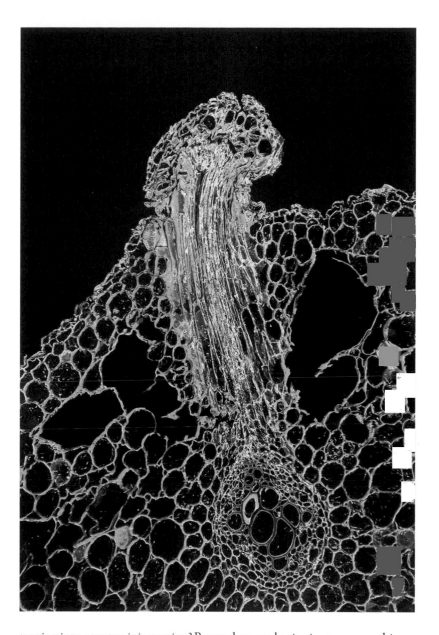

turning into a root as it is growing? Researchers are beginning to answer this by looking at how master genes control each other's activity to 'lock' particular combinations into place, and how certain master genes are held either 'on' or 'off' by the ways cells modify their chromosomes.

Interestingly, biologists studying the formation of animal embryos have shown that animals also rely on relatively small numbers of master genes to control their development. Mutations to these genes can have similarly dramatic effects: for example, transforming the antennae of fruit flies into legs. Scientists believe that the last common ancestor of animals and plants was a single-cell organism living somewhat over 1.5 billion years ago. Many of the master genes that control development in the two kingdoms belong to related gene families, indicating that they were ultimately inherited from the single-celled, common ancestor. Therefore, although plants and animals

evolved into their multi-cellular forms separately, they both began with a similar genetic toolkit to control cell behaviour. Presumably, in some ancient ocean, the master genes helped the common ancestor to regulate its single-celled lifestyle.

SENSITIVE ARCHITECTURES

To understand plant development fully, researchers need to go beyond discovering how each part of the plant constructs itself: they must also find out what controls when, where and how many parts are made, i.e. the plant's overall architecture and how it changes through time. It is these factors that are responsible for much of the diversity of plant forms. Sunflowers, for example, concentrate their growth into a single main shoot lifted high on a long stem. In contrast, grasses keep most of their shoots at ground level—only sending leaves up into harm's way—and readily activate the growth of new shoots to develop into a thick, low growing mat.

For researchers interested in plant architecture, the timing and arrangement of flowers is particularly significant. Of major importance is whether a plant flowers just once and then dies (annual and biennial species), or flowers over many years (most perennial species). Flowering patterns are also crucial for crop plants. For example, wild relatives of cereals hedge their bets by flowering and producing seeds over an extended period—a good option given the constant risk of being grazed to ground level by passing herbivores. Farmers, however, need cereals that flower and can be harvested in one go. As prehistoric peoples selected plants with the largest yield at harvest time, they created crops with new growth patterns. Hence unlike their wild relatives, wheat and rice initiate of all their flowering stems in one flush early in their growth, resulting in seed heads that mature simultaneously.

From the decision to germinate onwards, each plant fits its development to its own particular environment and life history. Consequently, plant architecture can vary dramatically even between genetically identical individuals. Not surprisingly, for example, plants detect light, monitoring the intensity, direction, duration and aspects of the colour of the illumination they receive. As anyone who has grown plants on a windowsill

Above
Cress seedlings' responses to uniform light (left), continual darkness (centre) and undirected light (right).

Opposite
Twin trees showing a branching response to mutual shade.

knows, once the seedling appears it bends towards the light (detecting its direction), doing so more when the overall light intensity is low. More subtly, by comparing the length of daylight with their own internal clock, plants match when they produce new leaves or come into flower to the seasons of the year. Plant's ability to detect temperature assists this process.

Apart from the effects of detecting light, much of the shape of a plant depends on its responses to gravity. For most plants, the main shoot grows up and the main root down, but shoot branches, root branches and, of course, leaves normally grow closer to the horizontal—allowing the plant to explore the space around it. Plants also detect other forces. If they are regularly shaken by the wind, plants grow shorter, thicker stems and make smaller leaves. Climbing plants wrap stems or tendrils around supports by detecting touch. Plants even respond to their own weight, thickening branches as they grow to support their increased size.

Observing how plants adapt their development to their environment shows that plants don't use each piece of environmental information in isolation. This is clear to see in how the combination of gravity and light can affect the angle of branches growing from the main shoot—on many plants, such branches grow closer to the horizontal in the sun than in the shade. Environmental information is also integrated with information about the plant's internal conditions. For example, plants match the growth of their root system to the availability of nutrients in the soil, producing new roots in nutrient-rich patches. However, this response is much stronger in plants that are nutrient deficient than in those that have been well fed.

A key challenge is to understand how and where relevant information is processed and decisions about the plant's future growth patterns are made. How plants make the decision to flower is a good illustration. The central factor is whether cells in shoot meristems (see above) activate the genes needed to begin the flowering process. These genes are controlled in part by information stored at the meristem, such as whether or not the plant has experienced winter. However, mature leaves lower down the shoot also play a role, sending a signal (a small protein called "florigen") up to the

Above
Farmed wheat plants initiate all their flowering stems simultaneously if planted correctly. This leads to sychronicity in harvesting.

Opposite
A collation of *Phleum arenarium* (sand cat's tail) plants by John Henslow, arranged in descending height order.

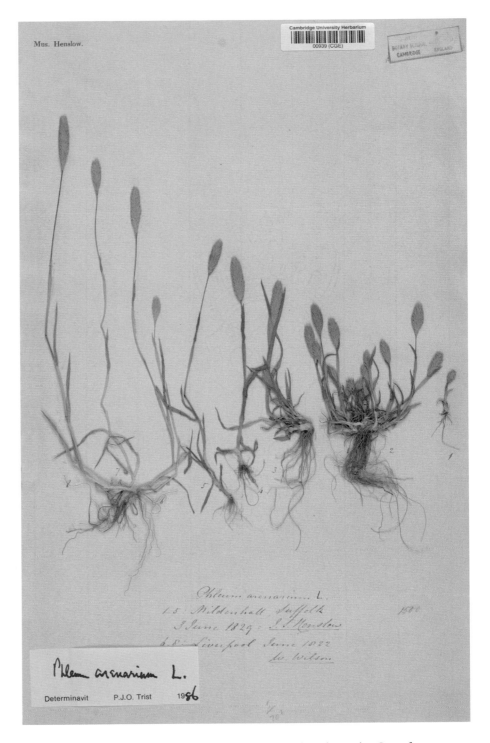

meristem to promote flowering when the day length is right. Once flowering begins, further changes are triggered. For example, when fruits start to form, hormones produced by the fruit are thought to inhibit other shoot meristems from making flowers—a way in which past decisions feed back on future growth (and why dead-heading your roses keeps them flowering for longer).

LANDSCAPES OF POSSIBILITY

Amongst the million plus of specimens in the Cambridge University Herbarium—now housed in The Sainsbury Laboratory—is the collection of John Henslow, Professor of Botany from 1825 to 1861 and the founder of the Botanic Garden. True to his time, Henslow believed species to be permanent aspects of Creation. As a good botanist, however, he also knew that plants within a species could vary widely in form, having different heights or branching patterns, or showing variations in leaf shape and flower colour. For him, this raised the question of whether it was possible to define the limits to the variability of a Created species.

To discover the answer, Henslow assembled multiple pressed specimens of individual plant species onto single Herbarium sheets—creating what he called "collations" to show variations between the specimens. For example, on some collations Henslow has arranged specimens according to their height at the time of flowering. From the modern perspective, Henslow's collations contain plants of the same species but that probably varied in both their DNA sequences (their 'genomes') and their individual growing conditions. Today's equivalent of Henslow's ambition is to predict using only an individual plant's genome, that plant's probable growth patterns in a range of different environments.

In some cases, parts of the answer are straightforward. If, for example, a plant's DNA sequence reveals a disruption in a gene required to produce flowers, then the plant is likely to have a flowering defect (as in cauliflowers, see above). However, researchers have discovered that patterns of growth

Right
Photomicrograph of a transverse section of an English oak (*Quercus robur*) stem. The photograph shows the xylem—the part of the vascular tissue that is responsible for the transportation of water and minerals up the shoot. The xylem appears here as yellow holes. The fine red lines radiating outwards consist of cells of horizontal 'rays', which distribute water radially across the stem and also act as storage centres for starch and lipids. The cells in the roundish area at the left are pith cells.

Opposite
Oak tunnel with Spanish moss at the Botany Bay Plantation, Edisto Island, South Carolina.

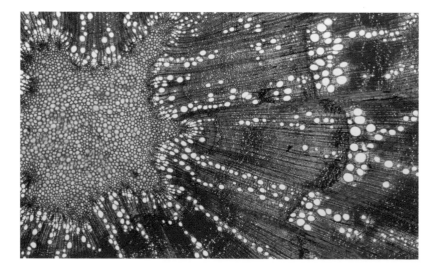

are often also influenced by large numbers of genes that individually have only small effects but that collectively cannot be ignored. A good illustration is provided by a recent study of flowering by maize plants that identified over 50 separate sites in the genome at which variations in DNA sequence altered the number of days for which maize grows before beginning to flower. For most of the sites identified, changes in sequence affected flowering time by less than one day. Collectively, however, these sites can shift flowering by weeks.

Understanding the actions of the multitude of genes that have only minor effects on development is a massive task but fortunately one that does not need to be completed before the information is useful. Comparing the growth patterns of plants with different genomes is sufficient to link variations in patterns of growth with corresponding variations in DNA sequences. This is what was achieved by the research on maize flowering. The result is the identification of sites in the genome—'markers'—that can help predict how a plant will grow even though the functions of the genes affected by those markers are unknown. Such analysis is becoming a major feature of plant breeding—allowing resources to be concentrated on plants in each new generation that carry markers in their DNA sequences corresponding to the desired balance of traits.

A remaining open question, and one that Henslow would have appreciated, is why are some species of plants more conservative in their growth patterns than others? In general, species that live in moderate environments show more flexible, i.e. less predictable, development than species adapted to extreme lifestyles. For example, oak trees grow well both in forests and in the open but show different patterns of growth at the two locations in response to the amount of shade. In forests, oaks grow tall, slender trunks with few branches below the canopy; oaks in the open develop shorter, thicker trunks with low, spreading branches. In contrast, responses to shade are much reduced in plants specialised either to a life spent in the gloom of the forest floor, or to surviving in the most intense light (e.g. cacti). Why are the mechanisms that control growth in the oak tree able to produce a more flexible outcome, and is there a cost—do oaks make more mistakes in their development than cacti?

THE RESEARCH ENVIRONMENT

The Sainsbury Laboratory opens at a time when knowledge of the living world is progressing at an unprecedented pace and when rapid improvements in technology are transforming our ability to investigate, analyse and manipulate biological systems. Firstly, advances in laboratory techniques are allowing biologists to perform increasingly subtle and precise experiments. For example, inducible genetic manipulation lets researchers watch what happens from the moment they switch an individual gene 'on' or 'off', while live microscopic imaging allows the resulting changes to be studied at the cellular level as they occur. Simultaneously, increasing use of automation is dramatically reducing the cost and time required to collect very large quantities of data, such as acquiring and comparing DNA sequences from different organisms, or analysing large-scale changes in gene activity and cell chemistry. For scientists studying plant development, the result is not only an acceleration in their own research, but also in the progress of vital, related fields such as genetics, biochemistry and cell biology.

A major consequence of the wealth of information being generated is that biologists are being forced to change their approach to experimental data. For example, understanding the balance between shoot and root growth—an important aspect of plant development—requires that experiments on changes in gene activity at shoot and root tips are considered alongside research on the overall flow of molecular signals around the plant and data on how those signals change in response to the plant's internal condition and to environment stimuli. Such information is too complex to grasp intuitively or to analyse fully by studying static diagrams drawn onto sheets of paper. Instead, biologists are collaborating with computer scientists to generate computational models of biological systems. The aim is to discover how the properties of the system as a whole emerge from the actions and interaction of its component parts. Using experimental results to construct such simulations allows researchers to test and refine hypotheses about how the system functions, showing points of weakness or of particular interest to guide future experiments. (See, for example, "Phyllotaxy: Progress on Patterns".)

Many of the new technologies available to biologists are employed across a diverse range of research interests. Therefore, to maximise their benefits, the scientific community has established collective resources at the university, national and international levels. Researchers at The Sainsbury Laboratory have robust support both within the University of Cambridge

and in the Cambridge region. Computational facilities, for example, include the Cambridge Computational Biology Institute and the Cambridge Systems Biology Centre—both within the University—and the European Bioinformatics Institute, which is located nine miles south of Cambridge in the village of Hinxton.

As our understanding of the biological sciences grows, so do the opportunities to employ that knowledge to help achieve a sustainable, healthy way of life. Specifically, understanding and manipulating plant development will be vital to securing an adequate food supply in the face of a rapidly rising world population, a more variable climate and predicted limitations on resources such as water and fuel. Current research is particularly focussed on plant responses to unstable environmental conditions. This is in part because the high yields achieved by today's elite crop strains can be dramatically reduced by even short periods of drought or excessive heat. Often the cause is not physical damage but the fact that the drought or heat triggers an emergency stress response in the crop—the plants short-circuit their normal pattern of growth to rush into early seed production. In the wild, faced with competition by potentially larger and better resourced neighbours, this response helps stressed plants to produce at least some seeds before they die. In the more pampered environment of a farmer's field, however, it would usually be better if breeders could create crops that simply waited out the stressful period before resuming their normal pattern of growth.

Looking backwards through time, biologists are expanding their investigation of plant development to cover an ever larger range of species, including those such as mosses that more closely resemble the early pioneers of plants' move onto the land. Through this approach, researchers hope to trace the innovations that allowed plants to evolve into their modern forms and so to create the environment that we currently enjoy.

Close up of a leaf from a poplar tree (*Populus* sp), showing the skeleton of vascular tissue that is left after the soft tissues of the leaf have decayed.

PHYLLOTAXY
Progress on Patterns

From petals circling a flower, to seeds packed around a dandelion head, to leaves forming in pairs, rings and spirals along a shoot, it is clear that plants are masters of pattern. Investigations into the mechanisms behind this talent provide a good example of how research into plant development can progress. Most effort has focussed on the arrangement of leaves around the stem, called the 'phyllotaxy'. New leaves form on the sides of the shoot meristem, a dome of cells at the very tip of the shoot (see main text). The most common pattern is a spiral with the angle between successive leaves up the shoot becoming increasingly close to the golden angle of approximately 137.5° (a mathematical concept derived from the study of ratios).

Early surgical experiments showed that cutting into the meristem to isolate a new leaf could disturb this trend towards mathematical perfection. After such experiments, subsequent leaves would form closer than normal to the isolated leaf. The obvious conclusion was that existing leaves inhibited new leaves from forming too close to them and that the surgery had prevented this inhibition. Geometrical calculations and early computer modelling—for example, in the 1970s by Graeme Mitchison, then at the MRC Laboratory of Molecular Biology in Cambridge—showed that such an inhibitory influence would be enough to generate life-like leaf arrangements, including the association with the golden angle.

Alongside the surgical experiments, it was also clear that leaf formation has something to do with the plant hormone auxin. Experiments in the 1930s showed that tiny drops of auxin placed on the meristem resulted in the growth of extra large leaves, or of leaves fused to their neighbours. On the other side of the coin, more recent research showed that chemicals that interfere with the transport of auxin around the plant could cause the growth of leafless stems. However, a drop of auxin placed near the tip of such bare stems could then induce a leaf to grow out at that position. Bare stems were also a feature of certain mutants of the weed *Arabidopsis* (thale cress) that prevented plants from making a protein 'pump' used to move auxin from cell to cell. So scientists knew that not only could auxin induce leaves to form, but also that normal leaf formation needed the ability to move auxin between cells.

The link between inhibition, on the one hand, and auxin, on the other was revealed in the last ten years with the help of advances in experimental techniques. Improvements in microscopy allowed researchers to study leaf formation up close in living meristems. In addition, scientists generated plants carrying hybrid genes that encoded the auxin pump protein connected to a fluorescent protein. The position of the pump proteins could then be traced by looking at the pattern of fluorescence. This showed that most auxin pumping occurred in the outer layer of cells of the meristem and also that auxin pumps were arranged to direct auxin towards the site of the next new leaf. Using a 'reporter' gene that had been designed to be activated by auxin indicated that this resulted in an increase in auxin concentration at the prospective leaf site.

Here was a link between auxin movement and leaf formation. Auxin was pumped to the site of the next new leaf and when the auxin concentration at that site was high enough, it triggered the new leaf to form. Crucially, by pumping auxin towards the leaf site, cells in the surrounding region of the meristem would partially empty themselves of the hormone. This could explain the inhibitory influence of existing leaves—by soaking up more than their fair share of auxin, new leaves would starve nearby parts of the meristem of the hormone and so prevent subsequent leaves from forming too close. Furthermore, observations showed that as each new leaf began to form, the arrangement

of auxin pumps in the centre of the leaf site changed to direct auxin down through the leaf into the stem below. From the point of view of the outer layer of cells in the meristem, it would be as if someone had pulled the plug. Auxin would now drain away through the new leaf, maintaining its ability to take the hormone from the surrounding region.

Researchers turned to computational modelling to investigate this process. Imagine the concentration of auxin in the outer layer of the meristem as contours on a landscape—with hills where the concentration is high. Cells pump auxin 'uphill' toward the site of the next leaf until the concentration (the 'hill') is high enough to induce the leaf to form. As part of the process, the auxin landscape around the new leaf sinks, preventing any other new leaves from forming too close. Using computational modelling to simulate this system shows that given a growing shoot with a supply of auxin in its meristem, the only rules needed are 'uphill' pumping, leaf initiation when the 'hill' is high enough, and sufficient auxin depletion around the base of each 'hill'. The critical point is that the effect of existing leaves draining auxin from their surrounding region always makes the site of the next new leaf into a high point on the auxin landscape. The 'uphill' pumping rule then directs more auxin to this site, making a mountain out of a molehill to induce that leaf.

Now researchers are hunting for the biological underpinnings of these simple rules. Why do cells arrange their auxin pumps to direct auxin 'uphill' and why does a particular concentration of auxin induce a leaf to form? More subtly, they are also looking at possible modifications to the model. For example, cells near the base of a new leaf can switch abruptly from pumping auxin towards the leaf to pumping auxin away. One hypothesis is that some cells pump auxin towards a leaf so vigorously that they severely drain themselves of the hormone and form a sharp 'ditch' in the auxin landscape. The 'uphill' pumping rule means that cells on the outer side of the ditch must now switch to pumping auxin away from the new leaf, creating a new auxin stream that will help determine the site of the next new leaf.

Purple coneflower (*Echinacea purpurea*). Regularly-arranged florets in the centre of the flower create a pattern of spirals that catches the eye.

PLANT SCIENCE AND THE ORIGINS OF CAMBRIDGE UNIVERSITY BOTANIC GARDEN

JOHN PARKER

INTRODUCTION

The Cambridge University Botanic Garden is the product of 170 years of close attention from scientists and horticulturalists. Each plant inserted into its framework results from a deliberate act, reflecting an underlying philosophy. If we gradually remove the layers like an archeologist, then the remaining long-lived plants themselves, when combined with documentary evidence, expose changing scientific ideas and attitudes through the generations.

Cambridge University Botanic Garden is a heritage site, designated not only for its age and beauty but also because of the successive impacts made upon it by eminent scientists associated with its foundation and its subsequent development. Its creation came from the vision of Professor John Henslow early in the nineteenth century, whose view of botany as an experimental discipline demanded a new type of Botanic Garden in which the plants were themselves the subject of, and materials for, scientific experimentation—"physiology", as Henslow called it. As the biological sciences developed here in Cambridge and throughout the world, so the Garden's design and collections were influenced by these new foci of attention, successively incorporating new ideas of genetics, ecology and, above all, evolution into its collections and displays.

From its inception, the academic function of the Garden was combined with Henslow's universal concern for education: this beautiful landscape was to be an invitation and encouragement for the whole of society, within the University or outside it, to gain knowledge of the world for personal advancement and self-improvement. This dual vision of research and teaching has been the driving force behind the evolution of the Botanic Garden for the last 165 years.

The historical context in this overview of the Botanic Garden prepares us for the next exciting phase in the life of the Garden. The creation of The Sainsbury Laboratory, in a prominent position at the heart of the Botanic Garden, and spanning the boundary between the nineteenth and twentieth century elements, will, through the plant scientists in the institute and their research on development, inevitably add twenty-first century insights to the continuing process of modification of this wonderful, historic Botanic Garden. The Sainsbury Laboratory and its scientists will transform our understanding of plant development, the Botanic Garden and its displays will present this new knowledge to everyone.

THE ORIGIN OF MODERN BOTANIC GARDENS

The Renaissance was born in the city states of northern Italy in the early sixteenth century. It promoted a new spirit of enquiry and investigation using direct observation rather than relying on the primacy of Classical sources. In medicine, efforts were made to understand the body as a machine through dissection, but a systematic knowledge of drug plants was also thought

Previous pages
View of the Limestone Rock Garden at the Botanic Garden, Cambridge.

Opposite
The original 1761 Botanic Garden at Cambridge, in a print of 1815 (detail).

necessary. The classical works of Theophrastus and Galen were evaluated afresh and collections of living plants for teaching were assembled in the universities, beginning with Pisa and Padua around 1540.

These plant collections were held in physic gardens. The herb gardens of monasteries were their predecessors but what characterised physic gardens was the systematisation of knowledge. Thus the drug plants were grown in beds with a common theme, such as treatments for heart conditions. Systematic beds have characterised botanic gardens since then but are now laid out according to a particular taxonomic system.

Physic gardens spread from Northern Italy to Montpellier, and then to Leiden in the Low Countries in 1583. The Earl of Danby visited Leiden on his Grand Tour, and on his return home endowed the first English physic garden in Oxford in 1621. It still reflects its Renaissance origin.

THE FIRST BOTANIC GARDEN IN CAMBRIDGE

Cambridge University failed to accommodate this new tide of knowledge despite stimulus from the English herbalist John Gerard. In 1584, Gerard wrote to the University suggesting a physic garden would greatly enhance its capability to teach medicine, and he would be an appropriate Curator. Several schemes subsequently emerged for a botanic garden in Cambridge, but it was 1761 before this came about due to the generosity of the Vice-Master of Trinity College, Richard Walker. He purchased the city-centre site of the Austin Friary and donated it to the University for a Botanic Garden.

The Professor of Botany, John Martyn, had been very active in medical and economic botany but Walker's donation came at the end of his academic life. He almost immediately retired and the Chair passed to his son, Thomas, who proved active and energetic, setting out the Botanic Garden as well as attending to his teaching duties both as Professor and as 'Dr Walker's Reader'. By 1770, a large plant collection had been assembled and a catalogue was published. Horticultural expertise was provided by Charles Miller, son of John Martyn's friend Philip Miller, Curator of the Apothecaries Society's Physic Garden in Chelsea. Not surprisingly, Cambridge Botanic Garden showed a striking resemblance to the older foundation in Chelsea.

Thomas Martyn lost interest in the University and its Botanic Garden after 30 years and retired to his parish in Bedfordshire. No botanical lectures were given in Cambridge from 1793 until 1827 and the Botanic Garden declined, unsupported by an academic environment: botany was in the doldrums.

A NEW BEGINNING FOR BOTANY

Thomas Martyn died aged 93 in 1825. The University immediately appointed the 29 year old Professor of Mineralogy, John Stevens Henslow, to the Chair.

Above
Professor John Stevens Henslow, the creator of the 'new' Botanic Garden.

Opposite
The collection of succulent plants in the Glasshouse Range in the late nineteenth century.

Henslow had taken a degree in mathematics in 1818. After graduation he studied crystallography, acted as Demonstrator to the Professor of Chemistry, examined the anatomy, taxonomy and ecology of molluscs, and carried out field geology by mapping the Isle of Man and Anglesey. Henslow was also a founder of the Cambridge Philosophical Society and acted as its Secretary for 18 years.

Henslow was a gifted teacher but little remained in Cambridge for a botanical course. He inherited a decaying herbarium assembled by the Martyns and had access to the run-down Botanic Garden. He called for help in teaching from his friend William Jackson Hooker, Professor of Botany at Glasgow University, to provide any illustrations he could spare. Henslow, however, was an accomplished artist and began preparing 70 elephant-folio diagrams for his lectures. His were the first illustrated lectures in the history of the University and were received enthusiastically by students. William Fox wrote enthusiastically in 1828 to his cousin Charles Darwin urging him to attend Henslow's lectures. Darwin was so encouraged by his eulogy that he took the botany course three times—in 1829, 1830 and 1831—but no others as an undergraduate.

Henslow found the physic garden at Cambridge "unsuitable for the needs of modern science". He required a large site, not surrounded by buildings and subject to fall-out from filthy coal fires, to enable a large variety of tree species to be grown for experiment and teaching; trees had been a neglected life-form in physic gardens. Henslow here marks a profound philosophical shift from the concept of a physic garden as an adjunct to medicine towards a collection held for the study of plants for their own sakes as the dominant

living organisms on earth. This reflects Henslow's own inclination towards biogeography and what would later become ecology.

A site was identified by Henslow less than one mile south of the City centre. This comprised 40 acres (17 hectares) of cornfields between Trumpington Road and Hills Road. It was bordered on the west by Hobson's Conduit, a source of spring water channelled from the Gog Magog hills to the south. A plan was commissioned in 1830 from Edward Lappidge, a London architect and landscape designer then working locally. It incorporated elements suggested by Henslow: systematic beds, a lake, a large lawn with imposing glasshouses, and a surrounding array of trees. The fields were owned by Trinity Hall and an Act of Parliament in 1831 was required to transfer ownership to the University.

Construction, however, was impeded for 14 years by the agricultural tenant, Mrs Bullen. She was not prepared to surrender the lease on the terms offered, so the site remained agricultural until expiry of the lease in 1844; Henslow's vision was temporarily frustrated. By 1844, the situation for the University and for Henslow had changed. Henslow now resided in Hitcham in Suffolk, having moved there as Rector in 1839. He visited Cambridge infrequently but still delivered his five-week botany course every summer. The University feared that Lappidge's scheme would prove too costly, so only the western half of the site was committed to the Botanic Garden; the eastern portion would be retained to generate income for its maintenance.

The University set up a Syndicate for the management of the Garden under the Vice-Chancellor, which appointed Andrew Murray from Liverpool Botanic Garden as Curator. Murray drew up a plan including the elements of the Lappidge scheme, but rearranged and reduced to half size. Construction began in 1846 when the Vice-Chancellor Ralph Tatham planted the first tree. Murray's plan, incorporating Henslow's requirements for 'modern science', has remained largely unaltered and is the western half of the Botanic Garden.

Above
Aerial view of the curving and irregular Systematic Beds in the western part of the Botanic Garden.

Opposite
The Lake in the western part of the Botanic Garden. The western area has remained largely unchanged since Murray's original plan.

ANDREW MURRAY'S DESIGN

Murray's design for the Garden is nearly symmetrical, bisected by a straight east to west axis leading from a gate on Trumpington Road. This imposing avenue is lined by Gymnosperms (coniferous trees) only—pines, cedars and redwoods. Around the perimeter of the site is a sinuous gravel path. A curving walkway crosses the centre of the Garden (the Henslow Walk) and links the peripheral path from north to south, crossing the Main Walk at its central point. This divides the Garden into four nearly equal quadrants: the northwestern contains a horseshoe-shaped lake, the south-western the systematic beds, the north-eastern a large lawn, and the south-eastern a Pinetum with deciduous woodland.

The crossing on the Main Walk is the focal point of the Garden, set with four magnificent trees—a giant redwood (*Sequoiadendron giganteum*), two species of cedar (*Cedrus libani* and *C. atlantica*) and a Crimean Pine (*Pinus nigra* ssp. *pallasiana*). The Main Walk is today the only straight line in this Garden of curves although Murray's design had a path at right angles to it at its eastern end, giving a T-shape. This cross-path was removed in the 1960s.

The Botanic Garden design was influenced by JC Loudon and demonstrates the beginning of a very English style, referred to as "Gardenesque". This has elements of landscape, in imitation of nature, combined with displays emphasising the individual beauty of trees and shrubs, ideally with each specimen separate so that its growth form can be admired. The style also displays the art of the gardener, through its combination of fine specimens disposed amongst well-managed lawns and paths. Loudon (1838) remarked that the Gardenesque style "is more suitable for… botanists, rather than general admirers of scenery, as it is best calculated for displaying the individual beauty of trees and other plants…". This was highly appropriate for this Botanic Garden, whose function was for research and teaching in "the modern science of botany".

Between the perimeter path and the Garden's boundary fence flowering plant tree species in Family groups were planted. The families more or less follow the order proposed by de Candolle (1819), and their positioning around the periphery was fixed by the Vice-Chancellor's inaugural planting of a European lime (*Tilia europaea*) immediately south of the Main Entrance.

The systematic beds are a masterpiece of Gardenesque design. Systematic beds are traditionally rather severe and rectangular, with herbaceous species following one another in a linear array of families. In the Cambridge design, however, the beds differ in size and are irregular with curving edges, forming an intricate array. There is no more than one family in a bed but the largest families require several to accommodate their diversity of species and forms. There are 150 individual beds, with 100 families represented by about 1,600 species. The original design is essentially intact but has been slightly modified by the insertion of three families of water-plants which have been shown, by DNA analysis, to be the most ancient in the evolution of the monocots.

Opposite
Andrew Murray's original plan of the Botanic Garden, 1845.

Overleaf
View of the Main Walk with *Pinus nigra* (Black Pines); Spring Bee Borders in front of the restored Glasshouse Range.

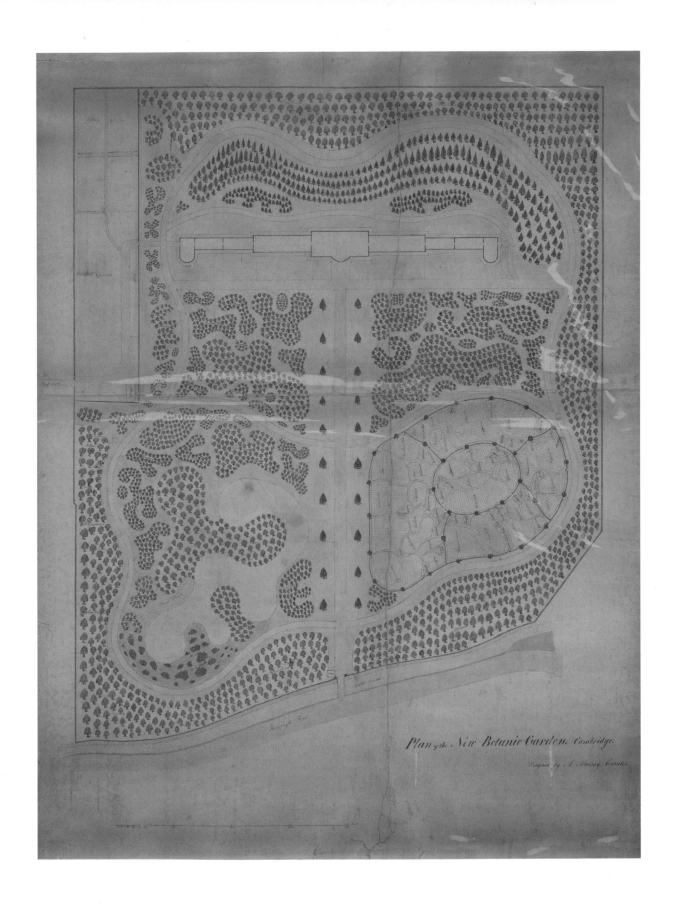

Plan of the New Botanic Garden, Cambridge.

The layout of beds follows de Candolle's 'natural' system of classification. This broke away completely from the Linnaean Sexual System, a purely artificial and pragmatic arrangement which grouped flowers simply on the numbers of their stamens and pistils, which dominated botany in England at the time. Henslow championed the Natural System and employed it in lectures and his *Catalogue of British Plants* (used by Darwin during practical classes).

The plan of the systematic beds is defined by low hawthorn hedges. In the centre is a large oval enclosing the monocotyledon plant families (monocots, those which have only one seed-leaf on germination). Monocots comprise about one fifth of flowering plants. DNA analysis has recently confirmed their common evolutionary origin. Four sinuous hedges lead away from this central oval, dividing the surrounding area into four unequal sections. These house the four groups of families into which de Candolle divided the dicotyledons (dicots, two seed leaves, representing the remaining four-fifths of flowering plants). The dicot families are laid out as they appear in his book, so those on the first and last pages are separated only by the width of a hawthorn hedge. The systematic beds, then, are a work of science but at the same time an enormous artistic installation—a representation of taxonomic philosophy using plants, beds and hedges.

HENSLOW'S RESEARCH PROGRAMME

The original trees in the Botanic Garden are a unique assemblage, since they illustrate Henslow's own research programme begun 25 years earlier. In 1821, Henslow had embarked on a major project: to assemble a herbarium (dried plant collection) of the whole flora of Britain. Henslow's collecting began in March 1821, reached a peak in 1826, and continued at a high level until 1831. Nearly 200 people helped improve his coverage of species and regions, and eventually Henslow accumulated 15,000 specimens from a British flora of only 1,200 species. Why did he build up this enormous stock of dried plants?

Analysis of Henslow's herbarium reveals his unique and individual scientific approach. He considered the species problem to be the most important question in biology, and searched for ways to address it experimentally. He had become completely obsessed by patterns of variation in nature and he used these patterns to define the "nature and limits of species". His approach was essentially statistical, based on many individuals and many populations. He arranged his specimens in patterns on herbarium sheets, unlike any of his contemporaries, displaying the plants as arrays of variants, usually based on size-differences or growth-characteristics. Henslow referred to this compilation process as collation. Through collation, he assembled visual patterns of natural variation, and on these he based his definition of species.

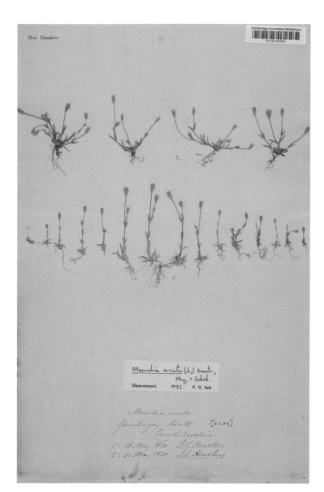

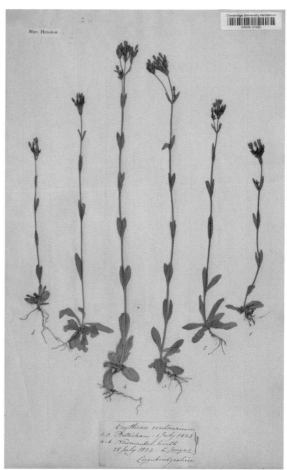

Henslow also devised a test, employing hybridisation, to distinguish patterns of variation characterising varieties of a single species from those which reflected distinct species. Thus, if hybrids failed to form, or were completely sterile, then the two entities were species; however, if hybrids were fertile they were only varieties of a single species. This distinction, based on breeding, became prominent in the mid-twentieth century, from evolutionary studies of animals undertaken by Dobzhansky and Mayr, who referred to it as the "biological species concept". Henslow also expanded his thinking on hybridisation to speculate that the laws of heredity might be deduced from comparisons "of 100 such hybrids".

Sudden changes of plant form occur spontaneously in nature, and Henslow referred to these as 'monstrosities'. He wrote papers on the development of monstrous flowers of *Adoxa moschatellina* and *Reseda lutea*, and speculated on their relationship to normal flowers and also to leaves. His herbarium contains about 100 sheets of these floral aberrations.

These three approaches to the species problem were transmitted by Henslow to his eager student Charles Darwin and gave him the intellectual framework from which to develop his own later thinking *On the Origin of Species*.

Examples of collation by Henslow, showing plant specimens arranged in distinct patterns of variation on his herbarium sheets.

PLANTING IDEAS:
HENSLOW'S RESEARCH PROGRAMME IN THE TREES

Remarkably, trees in the Botanic Garden demonstrate these three elements of Henslow's research on species. Thus, on the Main Walk, four subspecies of *Pinus nigra* from different geographical regions are displayed together. The most extreme morphological types are opposite one another: *P. nigra* ssp. *nigra* (Austrian pine) from Central Europe and *P. nigra* ssp. *salzmannii* (Salzmann's pine) from Mediterranean Spain. The Austrian pine has spindly, downward-directed branches bearing terminal clusters of short, stiff needles, while Salzmann's pine has massive, upwardly-directed, branches scattered with bunches of long, flexuous needles. These two distinctive forms are linked by fertile intermediates, and so are presented together as variants of a single species. They are living 'collation' patterns, like those on his herbarium sheets. At the crossing of the Main and Henslow Walks is a pair of cedars we call *Cedrus libani* and *C. atlantica*. For Henslow, they were varieties of one species based on his criterion of hybridisation and fertility. The same pair of cedars was also planted at the north-eastern corner of the Garden; sadly, one tree had to be felled after snow damage in 2010.

Other tree groups emphasise Henslow's obsession with variation. East of the Glasshouse Range are three distinct yews (*Taxus baccata*)—red-fruited, yellow-fruited, and the pendulous variety 'Dovastoniana'; a further clump of four varieties is located near the Rock Garden. Interestingly, all mature specimens of horse-chestnut, *Aesculus hippocastanum*, in the Garden are individually identifiable from leaf and fruit characters.

Henslow's fascination with monstrosity is illustrated by a cluster of beech trees, *Fagus sylvatica*, located within the family *Fagaceae* on the eastern periphery of his Garden. One is a standard beech, the second a weeping form, and the third a superb cut-leaved beech, *F. sylvatica* 'asplenifolia'. Nearby are groups of parents and hybrids in plane trees (*Platanus*) and oaks (*Quercus*)—the third strand of Henslow's research programme. There were probably many other thematic plantings but sadly there are no written records of them. The planting scheme was probably destroyed when Andrew Murray died in 1850, only four years after planting began, from pneumonia contracted after falling into Hobson's Conduit.

RICHARD LYNCH, ECOLOGY, AND
THE BIRTH OF MODERN GENETICS

After Henslow's death in 1861, the scientific direction of the Botanic Garden diminished. His successor was Charles Babington, one of Henslow's first botany students, who had overseen the Garden's development in the 1840s during Henslow's long absences. As Professor, though, Babington retreated

Canopy of the Weeping Beech (*Fagus sylvatica*) in the Botanic Garden.

into herbarium taxonomy and took no interest in the Garden. Its fortunes revived, however, due to a brilliant Curator, Richard Irwin Lynch.

Lynch trained at the Royal Botanic Gardens, Kew, and brought great horticultural expertise and vision with him. He carried out horticultural experiments, such as on cold hardiness, and also had an excellent eye for the impact of plants in landscapes. Lynch established plant collections—his succulents were famous—and constructed new features such as a rock garden. He added to the tree collection and in 1915 published the first authoritative account of it in the *Journal of the Royal Horticultural Society*. He also organised the Garden as a massive supplier of teaching material from the glasshouses and cultivated plots: over 100,000 specimens were supplied to the Botany School annually by the turn of the century. More importantly, Lynch accommodated the research requirements of Cambridge scientists.

Lynch's interests in the relationship between plant cultivation and environment led him to Arthur Tansley in the Botany School, founding father of British plant ecology. This left its mark on the Garden, as the nineteenth century focus on species shifted under Lynch into a concern with combinations of plants in thematic relationships. Demonstration beds were established to illustrate habitats and he modified or designed horticultural practices to ensure their successful cultivation. For example, a collection of maritime shingle plants was irrigated with sea-water. Lynch's legacy can be seen today in displays of local landscapes and their floras—fens, chalk grassland, arable fields, Breckland heaths—as well as in the long-grass areas he created, which help maintain the diversity of the Garden's flora and its associated fauna.

Lynch also appreciated the emerging needs of William Bateson for his research on the nature of heredity. Bateson was a zoologist and a committed Darwinist. He understood that the main weakness in Darwin's evolutionary theory was the lack of a sound understanding of heredity. Like Henslow 60 years earlier, Bateson realised that variation was the key. He published a massive zoological tome in 1895 called *Materials for the Study of Evolution* in which he considered "how have living things become what they are, and what are the laws which govern their forms?" For research, however, he turned to plants, and by 1897 was allocated one of the allotments in the Botanic Garden by the Botanic Garden Syndicate, as long as it was only for experimentation. Bateson and his technically skilled collaborator, Miss Edith Saunders of Newnham College, were supported by the Royal Society through its Committee on Evolution.

Bateson described "Mendelian" methodology in 1899, a year before the rediscovery of Mendel's work, and by 1902 Mendelian segregations had been demonstrated in the Botanic Garden for fruit colour in deadly nightshade (*Atropa belladonna*), hairiness in red campions (*Silene dioica*), and flower colour in sweet peas (*Lathyrus odoratus*). He expanded onto other allotments,

View of the Limestone Rock Garden.

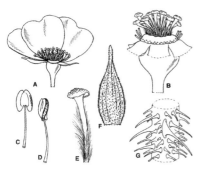

and persuaded Lynch to supply a glasshouse for closer control of crosses. Bateson coined the word "genetics" for this new study, and attracted other Cambridge scientists to him such as RH Biffen and RC Punnett (later famous for the "Punnett Square" and for stimulating the mathematician GH Hardy to consider gene fates across generations—the 'Hardy-Weinberg equilibrium'). Biffen successfully applied Bateson's experimental procedures to variants of bread wheat, *Triticum aestivum*. The economic importance of these studies led to the creation of a government-funded Plant Breeding Institute nearby in Trumpington village, with Biffen as its first Director.

Lynch was himself drawn into experimental genetics, and presented papers on hybridisation at the 3rd International Genetics Congress organised by Bateson in Cambridge in 1905. An enthusiastic collaborator of Bateson was CC Hurst, a landowner from Leicestershire, who applied Mendelian techniques to racehorses and orchids. Later, he worked in the Botanic Garden for 25 years, uncovering the origins of the garden roses by combining genetic and chromosome techniques. His collection of *Rosa* species and primary hybrids is still grown, with a display illustrating his findings. Hurst named two beautiful hybrids after the Garden—*Rosa x pteragonis* 'Cantabrigiensis' and *R.* 'Cantab'.

Edith Saunders not only worked with plants but also began a fruitful study of variation in chickens. She continued studying floral development, and particularly the ovary of Cruciferae, in the Botanic Garden until 1934, nearly 25 years after Bateson had left to become the first Director of the John Innes Institute.

EXTENDING THE BOTANIC GARDEN

In 1919 the University created an academic post of Director of the Botanic Garden, supported in horticulture by a Superintendent. Humphrey Gilbert-Carter, a taxonomist and eccentric but charismatic scholar, was appointed. He wrote the first comprehensive guide to the Garden in 1921. The cost of this curious and idiosyncratic publication (including plant names and quotations in Hindi, Arabic, Greek and Latin) was borne by Reginald Cory, a Cambridge graduate who loved the Botanic Garden and supported it financially throughout his life.

Cory provided funds to build Cory Lodge in 1926 as the residence for the Garden's Director. The house was designed by MH Baillie Scott in a charming neo-Georgian style, although its roots lie in the Arts and Crafts Movement. It has a C-shaped plan, emphasising the relationship between a house and its garden, following the precepts developed by Lutyens and Jekyll 30 years earlier. Cory Lodge became the Garden offices in 1986.

Reginald Cory died in 1934 and left his fortune of £200,000 to the University, solely for the benefit and development of the Botanic Garden.

Today, the Cory Fund is the largest trust held within the University, and is essential for the Garden's maintenance as a world-class institution. It was not used extensively until 1951, although many of the exquisite, rare books in the Cory Library were purchased earlier. In 1951, however, the experimental taxonomist, philosopher and humanist John Gilmour succeeded Gilbert-Carter, and immediately began a major expansion programme.

The eastern Botanic Garden land had been maintained as allotments since 1831. Gilmour incorporated it, effectively doubling the Garden's size. Most of the land was for public access, but the opportunity was taken to upgrade the Garden's working facilities. The private area was increased and became focussed centrally on the northern boundary. From here a promontory of land projected into the public Garden, with Cory Lodge marking its southern boundary. The first research building in the Garden's life, the Cory Laboratory, was built in 1957, and this was surrounded by research glasshouses, a frameyard, and experimental beds.

Experimental research on evolution and ecology expanded under Gilmour and his successor, Max Walters, along with a growing awareness of the need for plant conservation. Collections whose germplasm could be used for breeding and experimental investigation were brought together. The concept of National Collections began in the Botanic Garden with the gift of 80 *Tulipa* species from Sir Daniel Hall, Director of the John Innes Institution, in 1948.

The demands made on the Botanic Garden by scientists have changed considerably over the years. The requirement for field-scale cultivation has gradually diminished while the need for ever-tighter control of environmental variables in experiment has grown. Initially, this was satisfied by experimental glasshouses, but this degree of control is no longer sufficient. In 2005, growth rooms and growth chambers were installed in a purpose-built Plant Growth Facility in the Garden's working area, with more in the basement of the new glasshouse building constructed in 2010 near the north-eastern boundary of the Garden.

Above
Cacti in the Arid Lands display
in the Glasshouse Range.

Opposite
The restored Temperate House, now home
to the 'Continents Apart' display of Southern
Hemisphere plants.

Opposite
An educational workshop in the
Temperate House.

Overleaf
View of the renovated Terrace Garden,
representing the flora of New Zealand;
A heteropteran bug atop a thistle in the
Botanic Garden.

USING THE CORY DONATION: THE EASTERN PUBLIC AREA

The eastern area developed in a piecemeal way without a master plan. A connection to Henslow's Garden was made by a sinuous path around the periphery and the continuation of the encircling belt of trees. However, strict taxonomic regularity was no longer maintained, although collections of *Alnus, Betula* and flowering cherries were planted. A majestic clump displays forest trees which were British natives in interglacial times but which failed to re-colonise after the latest ice-retreat. These 'Tertiary trees' are now mature—*Ostrya carpinifolia, Zelkova carpinifolia* and *Pterocarya fraxinifolia.* The eastern Garden also provides a haven for the *Populus* collection, transferred from near the lake when that area was ravaged by honey fungus, *Armillaria mellea.*

The centre-point of the eastern area is a curving grass path flanked by plant-rich grassland and mixed woodland. Scattered throughout are new botanical and horticultural demonstrations. They include: the Winter Garden, 1978–1979, a planned landscape, designed using plant form and texture along with colour of leaf, twig and flower, beautiful in the darkest days, a Scented Garden to enhance the range of appreciation of plants through senses other than sight, and a Chronological Bed, illustrating as a time-line the enhancement of the British flora which has resulted from exploration and exploitation of the world.

These thematic plantings illustrate twentieth century concern with pattern and process in plants and with the environment. Local landscapes and their floras have been created, a 'Dry Garden' established to emphasise water conservation on local and global scales, while a figure cut from the turf draws attention to the medicinal uses of plant chemicals. These break away completely from the species-dominated landscapes of Henslow's Garden. The new displays disseminate learning about plants in all their diversity of qualities and interactions, and interpretation makes them accessible to all.

A little of the Cory Bequest was used in Henslow's Garden. A large rock garden was wrapped around the eastern part of the lake between 1954 and 1957, requiring about 900 tonnes of carboniferous limestone pavement from north Lancashire in its construction, as well as some Wealden sandstone from Sussex. The limestone rock garden appears as a stepped rock outcrop on a mountain slope, a remarkable accomplishment in the flat lands of Cambridge. This was achieved by employing a dense back-drop of evergreens at the highest point, tricking the eye and brain. The rock garden is planted bio-geographically, grouping plants by their continental origins.

One feature in Murray's original design was never constructed—a north/south range of glasshouses terminating the Main Walk. In 1967, a fountain was commissioned from David Mellor, a silversmith and cutler of Sheffield, for this focal point. It consists of seven bronze 'water-lily leaves' rising from a circular pool. Each leaf emits a short, dense column of water from its centre. These reflect the towering, columnar masses of a pair of giant redwoods, *Sequoiadendron giganteum*, nearby.

Opposite
The bright orange stems of pollarded *Salix alba* '*Britzensis*' catch the low winter sun, here with yellow-stemmed *Cornus sericea* '*Flaviramea*', red-stemmed *Cornus alba* '*Sibirica*' and electric blue *Scilla*.

Overleaf
Children enjoying the Botanic Garden; View of the table-top pruned *Tilia henryana* (Chinese lime) on the public cafe terrace and across the new landscape by Bradley-Hole Schoenaich Landscape Architects to Cory Lawn.

TRANSFORMING TOMORROW

The Garden was transformed in the twentieth century by a donation from Reginald Cory. It has been transformed yet again by the gift to the University of The Sainsbury Laboratory. This magnificent building rises from, and complements, its beautiful surroundings. More importantly, the exciting plant science which is carried out in the building has its roots here in the studies of John Henslow and his ardent student Charles Darwin. At the same time, the entire functioning and visual aspect of the Botanic Garden has been touched by this development: there is a new, award-winning, main entrance at the corner of Trumpington Road and Bateman Street, the working area has been transformed with new facilities for the Garden and its staff and for growing its plants, while the superb Gilmour Suite, set against a new landscape, is a wonderful attraction for visitors.

Henslow's vision for a Botanic Garden "fit for the needs of modern science" was based around trees. An arboretum, he argued, would provide not only for the University but also for recreation for all. The Garden, then, has become a focal point of the community, offering public education—in the broadest sense and for all ages—through labels, lectures and literature, as well as via events and the Web, for about 200,000 visitors each year. In 2009, the first purpose-built classroom in the Garden's history was opened at Brookside and is integrated into an Education Suite. The Main Gate nearby is a fitting entrance to this living heritage site dedicated to universal education. The Laboratory's Gilmour Suite provides a beautiful cafe but also an opportunity to reach out to visitors—to give them an understanding of the work in the Darwin Herbarium in the basement below but, most importantly, of the scientists in their labs close by.

The Botanic Garden was conceived by Henslow to be a living exemplar of the "laws that governed nature" and he achieved this through the deliberate grouping of trees, and probably shrubs and herbs, which exemplify the lines of evidence which he believed would uncover these laws. Subsequently, the growth of the Garden in its first century reflected changing research concerns—the advent of genetics, ecology and experimental taxonomy. In the last 50 years, the focus has shifted to biodiversity, conservation and sustainability.

The next evolutionary step in the Botanic Garden has, at the same time, been revolutionary—the opening of The Sainsbury Laboratory. This will transform our understanding of plant development, using the power of DNA analysis, genetics and computation. Remarkably, plant development looks back to the Garden's founder, John Henslow. His concerns about diversity, development and the nature of species grew from his own background in mathematical and physical science, and were embedded in his experimental approach to biology. The possibility for resolution of his remarkable vision has had to wait nearly 200 years, for the opening of The Sainsbury Laboratory, University of Cambridge, in his beautiful Botanic Garden.

Opposite
Autumn view across the lake in the Botanic Garden.

Overleaf
Entrance to the Laboratory building; north facade of the Laboratory.

THE THINKING PATH: REINVENTING THE RESEARCH LABORATORY

Steve Rose

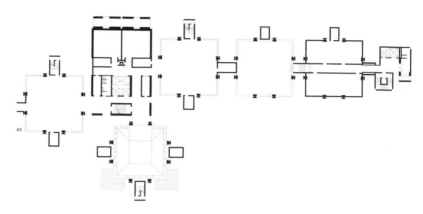

Modern architecture was greatly indebted to science, but it has taken some time to return the favour. In modernism's infancy, in the early twentieth century, it was advance brought about by science that enabled architects to give form to the spirit of their age. Liberated by the plasticity of concrete, the structural efficiency of steel and the economies of mass production, pioneers like Le Corbusier, Mies van der Rohe and Frank Lloyd Wright were able to pursue their progressive agenda, but they applied their genius primarily to established typologies: the house, the apartment block, the workplace, the city, and at a stretch, schools and hospitals. It was only later when modernism grew up a little, that it brought its sensibility to bear on the scientific environment itself. Even in the 1940s and 1950s, the science laboratories that had paved modern architecture's way, almost literally, were themselves dark, musty chambers, virtually unchanged since Victorian times.

One of the first architects to seriously engage with the laboratory as a design problem was Louis Kahn, with his pioneering Richards Medical Research Laboratories of 1957, at the University of Pennsylvania, in Kahn's native Philadelphia. At that time, the prevailing model for campus science buildings was a long, narrow block with small laboratory units either side of a central corridor, not dissimilar to a standard apartment block. By contrast, the Richards Laboratories provided large, open, generously glazed laboratory floors, closer to those of an architects' studio. These spacious studio-laboratories were stacked up in three blocks, served by external service towers containing stairs and services such as gas, water and ventilation.

The Richards Laboratories are today considered a key work of American architecture. Kahn's design was groundbreaking, particularly in its separation of "served" and "servant" space and its monumentalisation of the workplace, achieved in a unified language of prestressed concrete, brick and glass. But some of the building's details proved problematic. Scientists complained that the wall-free laboratories left nowhere to put equipment, or to obtain any privacy. They divided up the spaces themselves with partitions. Furthermore, the generous windows let in too much sunlight at certain times of the day, scientists complained. They resorted to sticking newspaper over the windows to block out the sun's glare, with Kahn reportedly visiting the laboratories and tearing it down, but eventually he conceded the point and designed some blinds. Another major problem, which has plagued laboratory buildings ever since, was flexibility. By placing the service ducts in towers at the edges of the floor plan, and making them only 18 inches wide, Kahn's scheme greatly compromised options for reconfiguring the open-plan labs.

Kahn addressed this lack of flexibility in his next significant laboratory design: the Salk Institute, in La Jolla, California, completed in 1965. The Salk deploys a similar architectural language to that of the Richards Laboratories, but the laboratories are smaller and their service spaces much larger. Full height service floors run above each of the three laboratory levels, which has made them far more adaptable to change (the building is still in use). Each lab space is also augmented by its own "retreat" or study space, detached from the laboratory. The Salk laboratories are an even more expressive composition: two sculptural, symmetrical blocks flanking an open marble plaza looking out over the Pacific Ocean. It is a postcard image of post-war architectural history, a powerful design that speaks of elevated, almost spiritual purpose. But while the scientists' technical needs were better met their social ones were not. They did not want to be sequestered in retreats; they wanted to be talking to each other. The building served to isolate them from each other when they would rather be brought together. The central marble plaza was an impressive gesture, but it did not function as a communal space. The real gathering place became the cafe and the outdoor area beneath it.

Refined though Khan's architectural treatment was, it set a precedent that few other laboratories could follow. By the 1970s, changes in the nature of scientific research were progressing more rapidly than architects had anticipated, and it was all most facilities could do to keep up. The space required for specialised support equipment and controlled environments—microscope rooms, cold rooms, dark rooms, tissue-culture rooms—started to increase. In the 1980s a forward-looking lab might have factored a ratio of 15 square metres of such support space for every 30 square metres of lab space. By 2000, that ratio was 1:1. A decade later, taking those trends into account, new laboratories were working on a ratio of 1.75:1. Also changing was the proportion of time researchers spent working in the laboratory as opposed to analysing data at their desks. 20 years ago, only a quarter of the working day would be spent away from the lab in this "write-up space", as it is called. Today, a researcher might spend three quarters of their time there.

As a result of these perpetually shifting goalposts, few laboratories have achieved a satisfactory performance for a significant length of time. More often than not, they were either designed with little consideration for their specific purpose, or in such a way as to be unable to respond to change. By the beginning of the twenty-first century, the typical laboratory building had become a confusing labyrinth of spaces, cluttered by ad-hoc additions such as ducts and pipes. And despite half-hearted attempts to address the social aspect of research communities, the result was invariably little more than a front-of-house atrium for public events, concealing a mess of working spaces beyond.

One person who has encountered many such undesirable research environments is Roger Freedman, the Gatsby Foundation's chief advisor in the development of the Cambridge building. Freedman was instrumental in the establishment of the Sainsbury Laboratory at the John Innes Centre in Norwich, and was an early advocate for the plan to build a new plant

science laboratory. "In the course of events, I see a lot of labs around the world. When the Cambridge facility was approved by the Gatsby trustees I assembled a list of labs working in the same general area—plant science, molecular biology—either under construction or recently completed. When I went to these places I would ask people working there, senior and junior, what they thought about their workplace. I wanted two bits of information: what did they do right and what did they do wrong." Freedman began hearing and noticing the same things again and again, and he boiled these down to three basic design criteria for the new Sainsbury Laboratory.

The first was that it make the best possible use of natural light. Kahn achieved this ideal at his Richards Laboratories and Salk Institute but alarmingly few buildings followed up on it. On his travels, says Freedman, scientists he saw working in one artificially lit basement laboratory reminded him of the subterranean Morlocks from HG Wells' *The Time Machine*. "Nobody should have to suffer that."

The second was that the building should foster a sense of community and conviviality: "A lot of what modern science is about is people working together. It's about teams of people, interactions, collaborations. There are lots of things you can do to promote that. For example, one of the curious bits of natural history about scientists is that they don't go up and down stairs. Basically people interact horizontally. We noticed this in Norwich, where the Sainsbury Laboratory is built on two floors. If you want people to talk with each other you should put them on one floor."

Big open-plan labs, such as those at Kahn's Richards Laboratories, did not reflect how people really wanted to work, it transpired. But make the labs too small and dispersed and people were working separately and not bumping into each other in an interesting, collaborative way. Other design alternatives have attempted to resolve the issue since, even a simple factor like the positioning of the coffee machine can make all the difference, it has emerged. But given the variable conditions and the generally unscientific behaviour of human beings, there is no optimal universal solution.

Freedman's third condition was that the building be flexible enough to accommodate as-yet-unforeseen changes in the nature of plant science. As we have seen, failing to do so can result in a steady decline in the quality of working conditions, and therefore results, and renovating laboratory buildings can be almost as expensive as creating new ones. "The science in the lab will be driven by curiosity, and research at the leading-edge of plant science is changing rapidly", he says, "and that means you don't know where you are going to be in 25 years' time."

This final point brings us to an important question: given the crucial importance of flexibility in such buildings, and the unpredictable future trends in these fields of research, why create a permanent, quality piece of architecture at all?

Above
Louis Kahn, Salk Institute, La Jolla, California, 1965. View across the court, looking west to the Pacific Ocean.

Opposite
Stanton Williams, The Wellcome Trust Millennium Building (Millennium Seedbank), Wakehurst Place, West Sussex, 2000. The entrance courtyard with planted parterres leading through to the winter garden public area and connecting to the landscape beyond.

One reply would be that in today's globalised research environment, a high-end research institution like The Sainsbury Laboratory needs to attract the best talent from around the world, which means competing with the best facilities in the world. The nature of The Gatsby Foundation and the wider attractions of the city and University of Cambridge undoubtedly sweeten the proposition, but ultimately, these highly talented individuals will be most concerned about the environment in which they are committing to spend long hours doing their best work. More than a recruiting tool, though, the building functions as a statement of the integrity and intent of the institution within. If The Sainsbury Laboratory did not commit to architectural quality, what would that say about its expectations regarding scientific quality?

That brings us onto the next important question: how can one design a building in which good science is produced? The above discussions identify some of the logistical and technical design challenges, but producing an environment conducive to good science is not, itself, an exact science. One must ask less empirical questions: how can a building make its users feel comfortable and happy? how can it inspire them? how can it give meaning to their work? how can it instil a sense of community? or to put it simply, how can a building make its users feel happy to be there?

Science cannot answer such questions, but fortunately architecture can. Stanton Williams formed in 1985 as a partnership between Alan Stanton—who had previously worked with Richard Rogers and Renzo Piano on the Pompidou Centre—and Paul Williams—an architect whose background lay in museum, gallery and exhibition design. As a practice, Stanton Williams could be categorised as continuing an architectural sensibility that runs through figures such as Le Corbusier, Louis Kahn, Carlo Scarpa and the Bauhaus, but their work has followed its own distinctive path, led by questions as to how qualities such as light, form, material and spatial relationships can combine to produce a building that is not merely functional but also enriching and uplifting. The result has been a portfolio of refined, sensitive, intelligent projects across a variety of scales and functions. A few are particularly relevant to The Sainsbury Laboratory. The Wellcome Trust Millennium Building, in West Sussex, completed in 2000 and commonly known as the Millennium Seedbank, is another high-quality research-based workplace with a demanding technical brief. Situated in a rural environment, the Millennium Seedbank also called for a balance between architectural presence and sensitivity to the landscape. Their earlier Compton Verney Art

Gallery was a crisp new addition to a listed eighteenth century country house, and demonstrated how modern architectural language can be sympathetic to a historic context. And urban projects like their House of Fraser department store for Bristol's city centre or Coventry's Belgrade Theatre, showed how a considered approach to material, mass and light can create a building that engages and integrates with the city.

Stanton Williams have a strong belief in craftsmanship, in the way things are made, in how the expression of a small detail can influence the whole. They have a sculptor's fascination with the way forms and spaces interlock, materials engage with each other—abstract artists such as Ben Nicholson and Eduardo Chillida are cited as inspirations as often as other architects. As a studio, though, Stanton Williams' success has been equally predicated on their ability to engage with their clients, and perhaps deliver them a building beyond their own expectations.

"One of the ways they really distinguished themselves to me was that they didn't turn up with a bunch of drawings saying, 'this is what it should be'", remembers Roger Freedman of his early encounters with the architects. "They gave time to studying the site. And they gave time to understanding what their remit was, what the building had to be in order to work as a laboratory. And it was only when they had digested those issues that they started sketching out general ideas. They shot up in my estimation because of that. They really listened."

"One of the great things about being an architect is that in every job, you are educated by your client, and in a sense you educate them about spaces and forms and scale and all the work that we do", says Alan Stanton. "So there is this wonderful thing about actually learning what they are all about, really absorbing it and becoming totally involved in it. Hopefully, drawing on the technical expertise around us, we brought a fresh approach to this laboratory building. We were not afraid to ask the naïve questions. In fact, this was an opportunity to rethink a lot of those questions."

"There are complex technical requirements but actually the heart of the building was the people", says Gavin Henderson, Stanton Williams' Project Director for The Sainsbury Laboratory. "How you promote interaction, how you create the right working environment. It is not about being specialists in laboratory design; it is about designing places for people to inhabit."

As well as Freedman, Stanton Williams' design team also benefited from the experience of Alan Cavill, consultant laboratory manager at the Sainsbury Laboratory in Norwich, who would go on to fill the same role in the new building, Stuart Johnson, Project Manager and funder representative of The Gatsby Charitable Foundation, and laboratory design consultant Robert McGhee, who had previously worked on laboratories designed by Cesar Pelli, Charles Moore, Robert Venturi and Denise Scott Brown and Rafael Viñoly. Having won a limited architectural competition for the project, the architects

Above
Eduardo Chillida, *untitled*, granite, nd.

Opposite
Aerial view of the Botanic Garden before construction looking north toward the city centre. The area of the Garden, comprising of horticultural and research facilities, is coloured pink: a site for the new Laboratory was identified within this area.

also took their own tour of state-of-the-art research facilities in Europe and the US, and like Freedman, they discovered that the majority had failed to achieve a clear internal organisation, and had become tangled mazes of corridors and equipment rooms. Paul Williams recalls that "the visits to the laboratories helped us to see how important it was to capture the appropriate sequence of work spaces required for the scientists: spaces for private thought, experimentation, discussion and debate, moving as it were from the introverted to the extroverted environment. How the scientists were going to experience and engage with the building had to be central to the design development. This was a primary concern." One of the better buildings that they visited was the Janelia Farm research campus in Ashburn, Virginia, designed by Viñoly, with McGhee as consultant, and opened in 2006. Consisting of single-storey laboratories laid out in terraced strips along a river bank, Janelia Farm is considered a standard-setting design, but it is a larger, sprawling facility in an isolated location. By contrast, the new Cambridge Laboratory would be a compact building on a site in one of the oldest cities in Britain: located within the Botanic Garden, on the edge of the city centre.

Historically, the site presented a series of intriguing contrasts. Here was a facility that would be operating at the cutting edge of plant science, extending knowledge into the future, but at the same time, it would continue and connect to narratives stretching far back in the past: the 250 year history of the Botanic Garden with particular relevance to Henslow and Darwin; the 800 year history of the University of Cambridge; and on an even broader scale, the history of science itself.

In these respects, Stanton Williams recognised that the siting of The Sainsbury Laboratory within the Botanic Garden was a great asset. In effect, the building is the contemporary counterpart to the Botanic Garden. Its laboratories, controlled environments and advanced technologies correspond to the systematic beds, carefully selected tree species and thematic landscapes laid out around it. "The Botanic Garden is a scientific research tool", continues Henderson. "And what we were building is also a research tool, looking at the same areas but with twenty-first century means. For us there was a connection."

The architects' initial visit to the site, one cold March morning, revealed the challenges and opportunities of the site. "The site itself was a bit like a farmyard", remembers Alan Stanton. "There were tractors, sheds, a few battered greenhouses, a little brick laboratory building coming to the end of its life." When Henslow first laid out the Botanic Garden here, it was a piece of farmland on the southern edge of Cambridge's city centre. Now the city has sprawled around it on all sides but the site, formerly a back-of-house area mid-way along the north boundary of the Garden, still had the quality of an urban edge, with a hard line of mews houses to the north and the tamed 'countryside' of the Botanic Garden on the other three sides. "We felt that the new building", continues Stanton, "could in some way respond to this 'edge' condition—the city to the north and the garden, as a kind of idealised countryside—to the south."

What also struck the architects, though, was the idea of a building arranged around a courtyard. "On our first site visit, Paul Williams and I began to discuss the idea of a courtyard building—to develop a form that could 'capture' the space of the garden and somehow connect the external landscape with the interior spaces of the building."

Since the Middle Ages, the dominant model for Cambridge's colleges has been a quadrangle design, of course, but the architects were not seeking to emulate this essentially inward-looking precedent. They were more mindful of the courtyard's associations with communication and circulation, as with a monastic cloister or a Greek stoa. The courtyard layout suggested a clear, open internal route, along which people might be able to run into each other, stop and talk, or spill outside into the gardens.

Above
Aerial photograph of the Laboratory site prior to construction.

As an additional, poetic connection between the building and landscape, The Sainsbury Laboratory was to house the University of Cambridge's Herbarium—a priceless collection of plants including those Darwin collected on his five year round-the-world trip aboard *HMS Beagle*, which were sent back to and mounted by Henslow on some 950 sheets. The Herbarium represents a historic bridge between the large-scale plant science of the Botanic Garden and the micro-scale investigations of The Sainsbury Laboratory. In their preliminary research, the architects had visited Down House, Darwin's family home in Kent, and they were struck by his "thinking path". Also referred to as the "sand walk", this was a circular path through a strip of planted woodland close to the house for the express purpose, as the name implies, of contemplative strolling.

Darwin's little piece of landscape design appealed to the architects since it brought together similar themes to those they were grappling with in Cambridge: engagement with nature, movement through a landscape, scientific contemplation, inspiration. Thus, the thinking path grafted itself neatly onto the designers' previous ideas of a courtyard layout as another way of ordering and animating the building, of forging connections between users of the building and members of the public (the building would also house a cafe for the Botanic Garden) and between people working in different parts of the building. Just as the thinking path had inspired Darwin, so it would inspire a new generation of scientists.

Clockwise from top left
Aerial view of typical college courts, Cambridge—Corpus Christi and St Catharine's Colleges, Cambridge; Salisbury Cathedral Cloister; Trinity College Library, Cambridge; Stoa of Attlalos, Athens.

Overleaf
Concept development sketches.

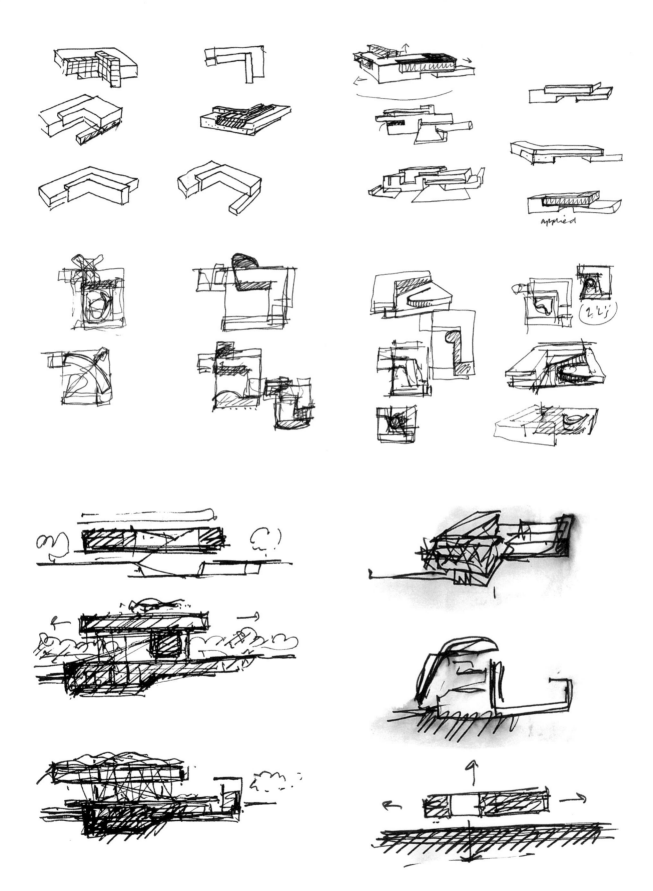

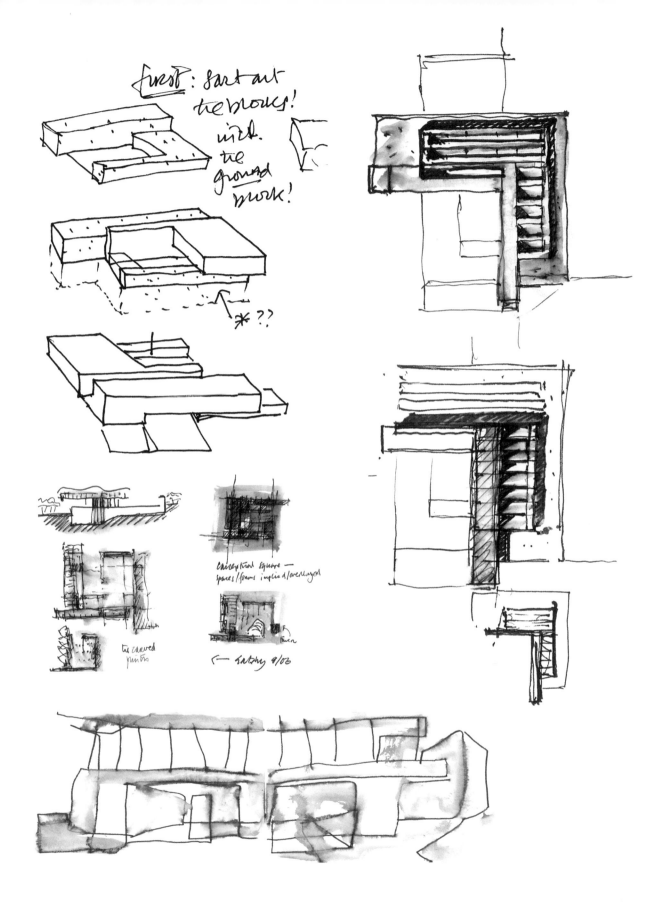

Initial attempts to arrange the building's accommodation into the desired courtyard form "squeezed all the air out of it", however. There was a great deal to fit in, after all. Stanton Williams had decided that the laboratories—and therefore the ancillary equipment rooms, write-up spaces and offices that went with them—should be situated on the upper storey of the building, so as to exploit natural light and to optimise communality (scientists do not go down stairs, remember). That left the ground floor for the building's more public areas: the lecture theatre and meeting rooms. The considerable volumes of mechanical and services equipment such buildings require would be tucked away in a large basement.

Like Louis Khan's Richards Laboratories and Salk Institute, the architects envisaged a substantial material presence for the building. Geological analogies presented themselves, of sedimentary rock, its strata exposed and carved by erosion. The primary material would be pale concrete but augmented with warm stone, quarried in Metz, whose honey yellow hues catch the light and complement the Cambridge cityscape. Alan Stanton also refers to Le Corbusier's monastery of Sainte-Marie de la Tourette, near Lyon, France, as an important precedent. Like The Sainsbury Laboratory, La Tourette, completed in 1960, is a traditional Medieval cloister reinterpreted as a cubistic concrete composition. Its two orderly upper storeys of monk's cells seem to float above relatively loosely organised floors below, as if to suggest a higher plane of rationality. The context in Cambridge, Stanton suggests, is not all that different: serried ranks of scientists and serried ranks of monks, both divining the workings of creation.

Looking beyond architecture, the aforementioned Ben Nicholson's carved reliefs, in particular, conveyed a similar sense of erosion and accumulation, balance and proportion, to what the architects were aiming for. Another talismanic image was Antonella da Messina's fifteenth century painting, *St Jerome In His Study*, which hangs in London's National Gallery. At the dead centre of this image, St Jerome sits in profile, absorbed in study in what appears to be an ergonomic Renaissance study carrel—an elevated, free-standing wooden construction that sits in the middle of a much larger space, the rural landscape visible beyond. Despite being more than 500 years old, this image spoke of everything the architects were striving for: an architecture based around the individual at one end of the scale, and the landscape outside at the other.

Left
Antonella da Messina, *St Jerome In His Study*, c 1475.

Right
Le Corbusier, Monastery of Sainte-Marie de La Tourette, Lyon, 1960.

Opposite
Ben Nicholson, *1939–44* (painted relief), 1939–1944.

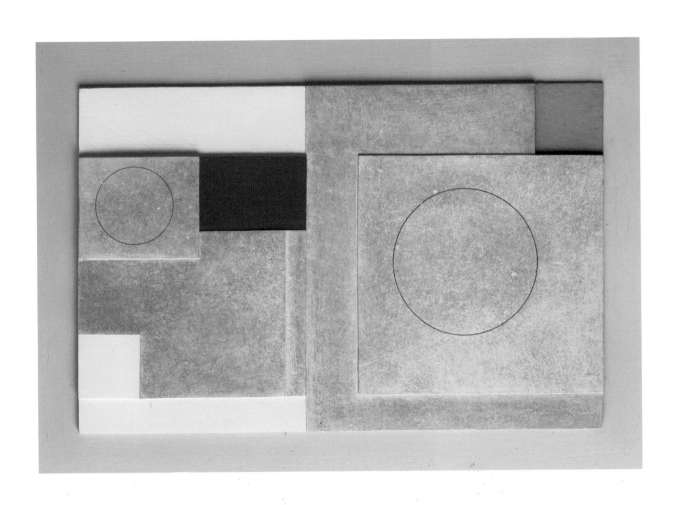

To see the result of all these concerns on the finished work, a good place to start is the northeast corner of The Sainsbury Laboratory. The main entrance is just to your right, while round the corner to the left you would walk down the side of the building to the Botanic Garden behind. The upper storey is clearly distinguishable from the lower by its regular ranks of stone columns, and the two are separated by a flush band of concrete that wraps right around the building. This "datum level" is something of a trademark in Stanton Williams' work. It serves to reinforce how the ground level varies in relation to the building, and combined with a parallel concrete slab along the roofline, it reinforces the allusion to the strata of sedimentary rock.

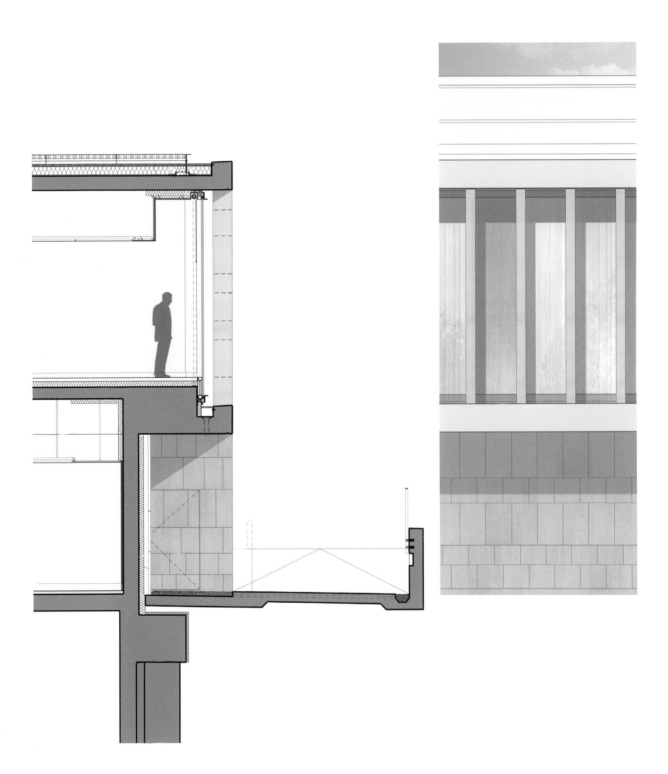

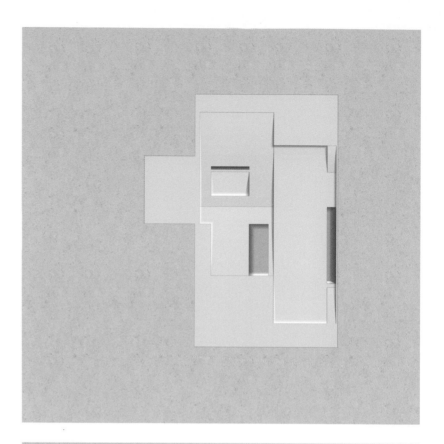

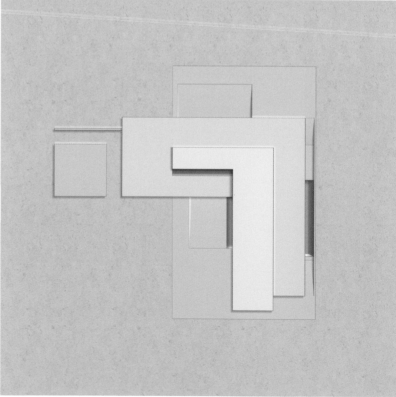

Right and opposite
Study models exploring treatment of the ground plane as a carved surface.

Overleaf
Entrance to the Laboratory; View of the Laboratory opening out into the landscape of the Botanic Garden.

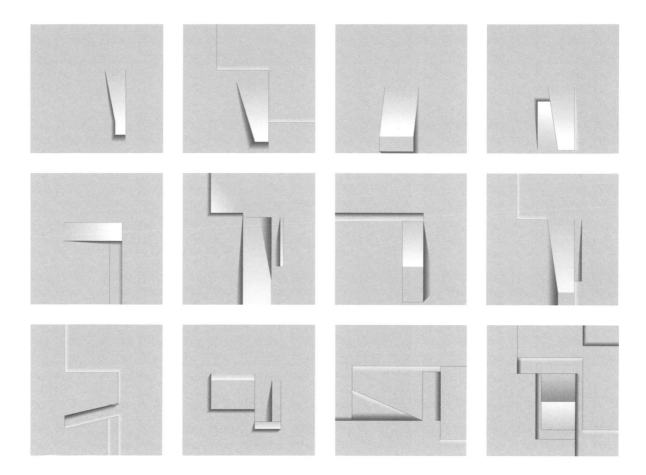

This corner is the only spot, though, where the two levels are in exact alignment, presenting a sharp vertical edge. As you progress around the building in either direction, the upper floor, the laboratory level, projects in bold cantilevers over the lower level, as if the building's base had been eroded away. Continuing the geological association, you will also notice that the ground level slopes down towards the entrance of the building. The whole structure is carved into the ground slightly. The overall impression is of permanence and rootedness (a third of the building is actually below ground). The embedding also lowers the height of the building, bringing it into a more equitable relationship with the mews houses bordering the site.

The rock-like mass gradually dissolves as you move away from this corner. The north and east facades present a solid, urban face towards the city, unified by the orderly stone columns, but by the time we arrive at the south side, this rigidity gives way to a looser, more rural order addressing the "countryside" of the Botanic Garden. The controlled lines break free in great folds of concrete, forming a single-storey cafe with a roof terrace above. And at the west side, there is no building at all. This edge of the quadrangle is formed by mature oak and chestnut trees, planted by Henslow some 160 years previously.

Either side of the laboratory building, that 'farmyard' of a site has been organised into a strip of functional activities along the boundary of the Botanic Garden—greenhouses, nursery gardens, bicycle racks, chipping and composting areas, a shed for equipment storage—a buffer zone between the city border and the Garden proper. Where this zone passes in front of the building, we find an orderly little grove of *Ginkgo* trees rising out of the paving—an idea inspired by the Moorish-designed Patio de los Naranjos in Seville Cathedral, the architects say, where a courtyard is planted with a similar grid of orange trees. This architectural planting signifies the building's botanical purpose and symbolically marks a fusion of natural and manmade orders. The *Ginkgo* trees also set up a subtle evolutionary narrative. *Ginkgo biloba* is the last survivor of an essentially prehistoric genus. *Ginkgo* leaves have been found in fossils 270 million years old. When we proceed to the building's inner courtyard, we find another, similarly architectural grove, this time of olive trees—a more modern, agricultural plant compared to the primitive *Ginkgo*. The olives might suggest a reinterpretation of Plato's original grove of Academe, a tranquil, organic heart of the building, and a marker of the organic content in the Herbarium beneath. Continuing this line through to the other side of the building, we find another, even more cultivated landscape space in the progression: the lawn outside Cory Lodge.

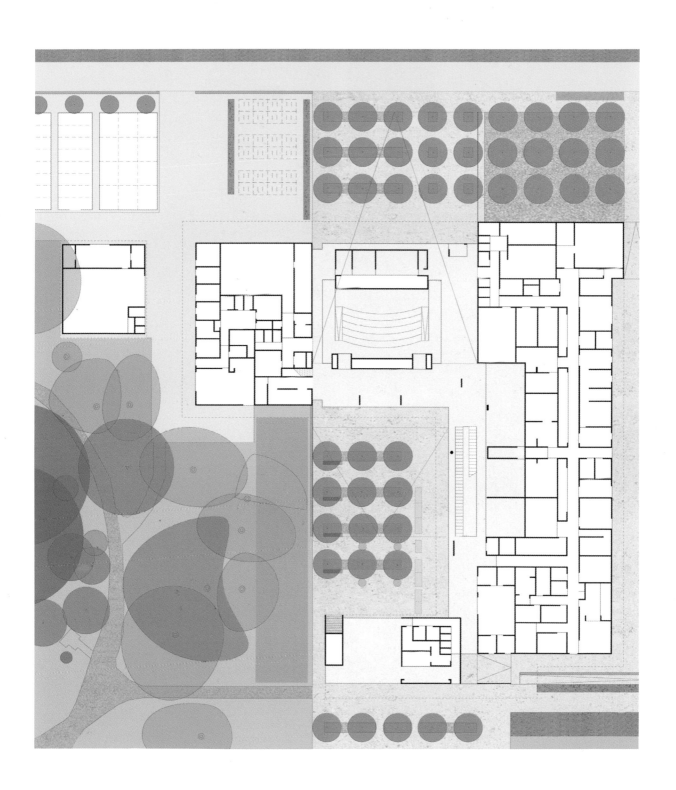

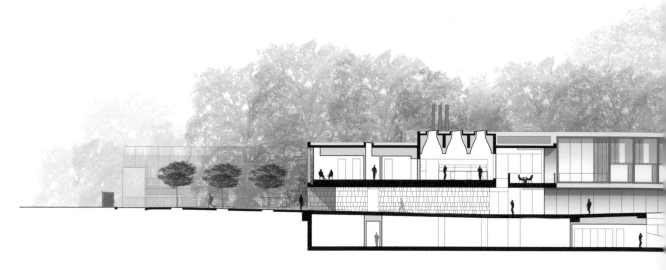

Above
Section through the building and courtyard.

Opposite clockwise from middle left
Timber formwork for the first floor concrete slab, illustrating the complexity of construction required to achieve the finished appearance; public cafe; laboratory; view from laboratory in to internal 'street'.

Overleaf
Coffers and lighting in the lecture theatre ceiling.

The primacy of the building's solid skeleton is apparent the moment one crosses the threshold. The most visible material inside is the same smooth, pale concrete we saw on the outside. All the fittings and secondary features—glazing, lighting, insulation panels, ventilation ducts—are consistently expressed as secondary additions, slotted into this permanent structure. Precise detailing and quality materials—oak, steel, stone, glass—add a sense of refinement, as does the spatial clarity. The effort that went into achieving this unity is entirely concealed, but achieving simplicity is always a complex process. The concrete slab bearing the upper storey, for example, appears as a simple band around the edges of the building, but inside it is more like a very deep aeroplane wing, with a complicated structural system of braces and cross-walls designed to bear the massive cantilevered loads. In places it is 1.5 metres thick. Users are unlikely to ever contemplate the difficulty of not just designing and casting such a slab of concrete but aligning it precisely with the concrete slab above and the stone columns on the façades in between. If one element was out of line, then it would be noticeable.

Above
Entrance foyer; lecture theatre.

Opposite
Staircase leading up to the laboratory level
and down to the Herbarium.

Overleaf
Staircase and central court.

Take a few steps further inside, towards the inside corner of the main L-shaped block, and the building opens itself up like a book. To the right, the lecture theatre is immediately visible through a glass wall. Even Susanna Heron's art piece—*Henslow's Walk*—is visible on the far side of the lecture theatre. To the left are the meeting rooms down the eastern flank of the building. In front, another wall of glass looks out onto the central courtyard with its olive grove, the public cafe beyond, and the foliage of the Botanic Garden all about. But the eye is also led upwards and downwards. Large voids in the ceiling beyond the lecture theatre offer views to the laboratory level above. From certain angles, one can even see into the laboratories themselves. And a staircase directly ahead draws you naturally upwards to the laboratory level, or down to the University's Herbarium in the basement.

Opposite
Internal 'street' with staff dining area.

This main staircase is one of the most important elements of the building (there is a secondary staircase to your right, at the western end of the building). It continues the principal route from the entrance upwards in the direction of the Botanic Garden, and it does so in a long, gentle slope. The rise, depth and width of its treads subtly dictates a steady, almost ceremonial pace, in keeping with the landscape, with the thinking path. Rather than a simple device for getting from A to B, it is a staircase on which one could stop and hold a conversation. Even descending to the basement, the staircase is more generous than one would expect, in deference to the significance of its contents.

Ascending to the laboratory level, one could continue in the same direction towards doors opening onto the roof terrace, overlooking the Botanic Garden. The thinking path has brought you out into the landscape, and stairs at the other end of the roof terrace continue the route into the courtyard or the gardens. Staying inside, the stairs also bring you up to the building's main arena of activity. An internal 'street' runs around the inner walls of the L-shaped upper storey, looking out onto the courtyard below. The laboratories themselves, two along each side of the L, are immediately visible though glass walls. This 'street' is almost expressed as a free-standing element, like a bridge. Supported on a few slender legs beneath, it seems to have broken free from the adjacent laboratories, opening up those voids we were looking up through into the labs just a moment ago. At its corner is the all-important coffee area, in full view of the laboratories.

Above
A view of the staircase from the main entrance leading up to laboratories, and out to the courtyard on the right.

Opposite
View of the stair and internal 'street' at first floor level.

Overleaf
View of the laboratories from the internal 'street'.

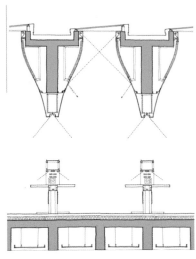

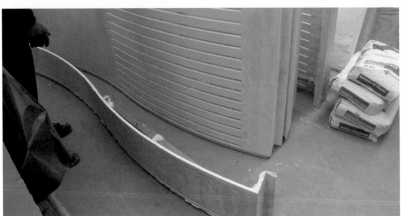

Design and manufacture of the roof lights.

Above clockwise from top left
Design sketch showing integration of natural and artificial lighting and air supply; full size study model testing integration of air supply and lighting; roof light structure; glass reinforced gypsum (GRG) sections of the finished roof light prior to installation; moulds for production of the GRG roof lights in the workshop.

Opposite
Laboratory roof light at night. The slots in the roof light conceal acoustic material.

Entering the laboratories themselves, the ambience changes appreciably. White curved 'beams' run along the high ceiling, and between them the sky is visible. Light is drawn down the curved forms to the spaces below. These 'beams' are cast from glass-reinforced gypsum with an internal concrete structure. As well as softening the natural light entering from above and allowing the spaces to be fully daylit through the majority of the working day, they discreetly house the ventilation ducts and artificial lighting. The workbenches are serviced from below, which makes for an uninterrupted, uncluttered space. It also means benches can be easily detached and moved, if necessary. The wall surfaces are all either white—made of the same cast epoxy resin as the workbenches—or bare-faced concrete. The feeling is calm, spacious, chapel-like—as if the scientific work is being celebrated, sanctified, even. But beyond, the rest of the building, the courtyard and the Botanic Garden are in constant view. The researchers are elevated but not isolated.

The other functional spaces organise themselves around the laboratories: two open-plan write-up spaces at either end of the L; equipment rooms, cold rooms and the like behind the laboratories; and along the two outward-facing walls, across an internal corridor, meeting rooms, private offices and further support rooms. The latter are significant. Behind the unified ranks of stone columns on the external facades, they can be broken up, joined together and reconfigured into further laboratories, spaces for unmanned experiments or extra write-up space, according to changing future demands. Again, a balance between permanence and flexibility.

Above
View of a laboratory.

Opposite
Support corridor.

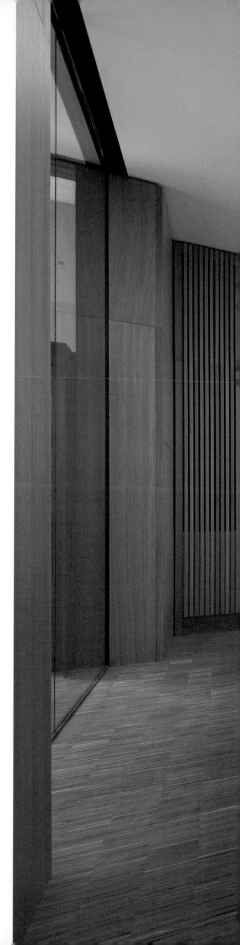

Opposite
First floor meeting room.

Overleaf
Detail of columns and glazing from interior.

ST ST ST

BOLT ON
HANDRAIL
✱ model

Opposite
Study sketches of stairs and screens.

Top
First floor courtyard facade study model.

Bottom
Full size mock-up of main stair to test size
and gradient of steps.

The clarity of The Sainsbury Laboratory's layout is self-apparent to its users, but for Stanton Williams it is the outcome of a long process of investigation and refinement. Modelling, in particular, is an important part of the architects' methodology—not just by computer, but in card, so the model can be picked up and looked directly into. Scores of models were produced in the course of the design process. Some major elements, such as the roof lights or the staircase, the architects even built full scale in their studio, just to make sure they were on track. "We have sat for hours, days, weeks over sketches, drawings and piles of card models, working our way through the spaces", says Alan Stanton. "Often we will take photos of the models, print them out and sketch all over them, drawing together in design sessions, asking, 'if you go up there, what will you see?' By the end, you can walk around the building in your head, so when you see it built on site, it should confirm what you have already created and thoroughly understood."

There are also touches that will go unnoticed by the majority of users, such as the difference in floor level between the laboratories and the internal 'street' they look out onto. The laboratories are deliberately raised up half a metre, not only to give scientists a clearer view of the Garden but also to create a difference in eye level and thus prevent them from feeling as if they are being observed like fish in a tank. Or note the way the ceiling height increases just a fraction on the wing housing the main staircase—establishing its precedence almost imperceptibly. "It is very interesting what just one step will do", says Stanton. "Just 150 millimetres will change your perception of a space and your relationship to another. It is a subtle move that people do not easily perceive or take notice of, but we are convinced people feel it."

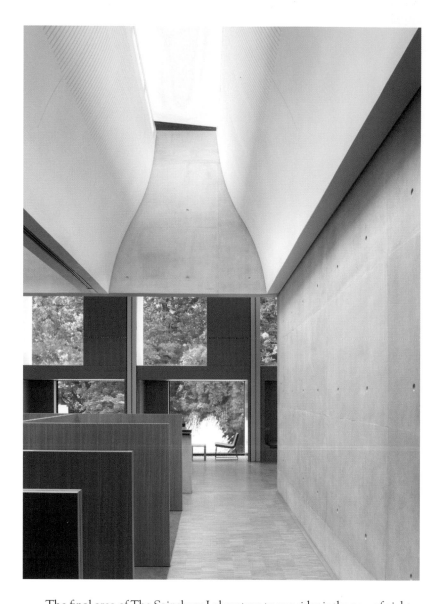

Above
Write-up area.

Opposite
"Study boxes" on the internal 'street'.

Overleaf
Central court with exterior facade of the
study boxes; view of the terrace outside
the Laboratory.

The final area of The Sainsbury Laboratory to consider is the row of eight open "study boxes" that run along the internal 'street', parallel to the main staircase. These are small breakout spaces, each containing a bench, a chair, a table, a whiteboard, and their own generous window on the courtyard. They are intended to be spaces where more intimate conversations and discussions might take place, where a couple of people might stray off the thinking path to further explore an idea. You could describe them as the modern equivalent of Saint Jerome's study carrel, or a reinterpretation of Louis Kahn's study carrels at his Exeter Library in New Hampshire—another Stanton Williams reference point. Kahn celebrated the simplicity of these spaces as the essence of architecture—a person, a wall, a table, a window—the minimum ingredients for an inhabited space. Likewise, The Sainsbury Laboratory's study boxes encapsulate what the building as a whole is striving for: individuals relating to each other and to the landscape. The purpose and inspiration for the project in close contact; a place for good science.

It might not be possible to gauge the success of The Sainsbury Laboratory for another 25 years, when hopefully its researchers will have made a tangible contribution to their field, but the facility is already along the path to achieving its scientific aspirations. World-class scientists have committed to relocating here, and those from other facilities who have visited have expressed their admiration, and envy. "A distinguished scientist told me that they were almost reduced to tears a couple of times when they went round the place—because it realised many things that they had only dreamed of", says Roger Freedman. "This place raises the bar. It treats the people who work here as human beings." It is not just the exceptional spaces and facilities of the new building, it is also the promise of the resources they need to perform their work: the financial support, the equipment, the freedom to follow their instincts.

If such standards are rare in science they are even rarer in architecture, say Stanton Williams, and for similar reasons. Just as the scientists have been entrusted with the latitude they desire, so the architects credit their clients, The Gatsby Foundation and the University of Cambridge, for giving them the freedom to fully realise their vision. "There has been a high level of patronage here", says Alan Stanton. "They had the confidence to bring in architects who did not specialise in laboratory design and they supported us to produce a fully integrated design. We have even designed the furniture in the offices, the signage, the typography. Often these elements are taken out of architects' hands at the very last minute, and they almost always detract from the overall intentions and lead to disappointment. This is what should happen but it very rarely does. It speaks of a client with a vision. A vision for science."

Above
Courtyard view of The Sainsbury Laboratory.

Opposite
The Laboratory viewed from the public area of the Botanic Garden.

Overleaf
The terrace of the public cafe.

MASTERPLAN

Construction of The Sainsbury Laboratory Cambridge required re-planning of the non-public areas of the Botanic Garden that are dedicated to horticultural activities and research. At commencement of the project many of the buildings and structures related to these activities had become redundant or were in need of replacement: the construction of the Laboratory provided the opportunity to replace horticultural facilities with new structures to meet the ongoing needs of the Botanic Garden, and to provide new research facilities which could be shared by the Botanic Garden and the Laboratory.

The completed scheme includes re-landscaping of the research and horticultural areas, an area of two hectares. This area is conceived as an ordered landscape organised by walls and hedges and contains new glasshouses, shade halls and a barn/equipment store for the Botanic Garden. A new research glasshouse and plant growth building provides growing areas for research. Plant growth rooms are located in a semi-basement below the research glasshouses, providing controlled environments which can be varied to replicate growing conditions appropriate to particular plant species or particular climate zones.

SUSTAINABILITY

The Sainsbury Laboratory Cambridge is a highly energy efficient laboratory building which has been designed for a long life, with a robust structure and a high level of adaptabilty for future needs. Sustainable buildings work well for their users and here great attention has been paid to the users' needs and to the quality of their working environment.

Technical aspects of the building's sustainability are carefully integrated into the overall design rather than being overtly expressed. Efficient heating, cooling and ventilation systems, together with high levels of insulation and air-tightness in the facades and roof, have enabled the building to significantly exceed emission targets set in Building Regulations and the energy rating

Top left
Research Glasshouse and plant growth building.

Top right
Aerial photograph of The Sainsbury Laboratory Cambridge, showing the ordered landscaping, horticultural and research buildings created within the non-public areas of the Botanic Garden.

Bottom
Equipment store for the Botanic Garden.

Opposite
Photovoltaic installation on the roof of the Laboratory.

targets for laboratory buildings. The Building Research Establishment
Environmental Assessment Method (BREEAM), which is the recognised
method of assessing sustainability, rated the building as "Excellent".

Particular attention has been paid to reducing the requirement for
artificial lighting. The main laboratory spaces on the first floor are naturally
lit through roof lights and are entirely daylit for the majority of the working
hours, with a hugely beneficial impact on lighting energy and the welfare of
the laboratory users.

Water use is a significant issue for both the Botanic Garden and the
Laboratory. Rainwater is harvested from the roof of the main building and used
for irrigation of the glasshouses and plant growth chambers. This approach
saves both energy and water as mains water cannot be used for irrigation of the
experimental plants.

On site renewable energy is provided by 1000 m² of photovoltaic panels
mounted on the roof of the laboratory, providing ten per cent of the building's
energy load.

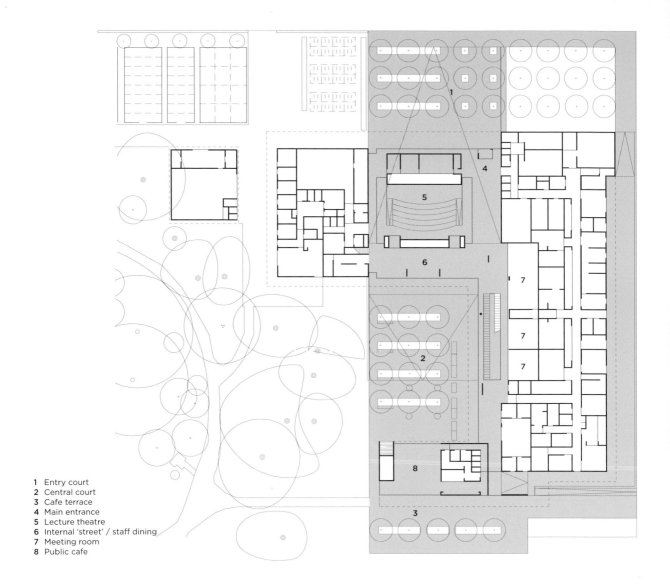

1 Entry court
2 Central court
3 Cafe terrace
4 Main entrance
5 Lecture theatre
6 Internal 'street' / staff dining
7 Meeting room
8 Public cafe

Above
Ground level plan.

Opposite top
First level plan.

Opposite bottom
Lower level plan.

Overleaf
Cory Lawn and public cafe.

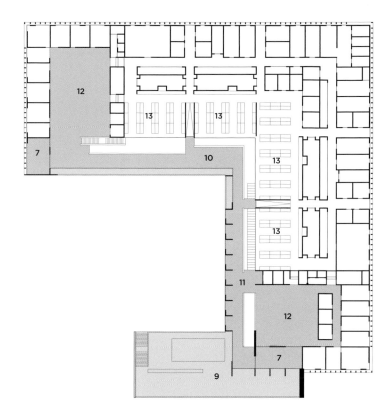

7 Meeting room
9 External terrace
10 Internal 'street'
11 Internal 'street' / 'study boxes'
12 Write-up and office areas
13 Laboratory

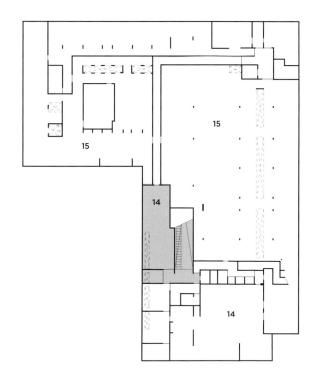

14 Herbarium
15 M&E Plant / Support Areas

GALAPAGOS
Norman Ackroyd

Painter and etcher Norman Ackroyd was approached by David and Susie Sainsbury to produce an artwork for the Laboratory grounds and subsequently sent to the Galapagos Islands to study the landscape there, using his unique ability to capture the spirit of a seascape. This visit coincided with the bicentenary of Charles Darwin's birth in 2009, and Ackroyd's journey to the Islands saw him following in his footsteps by embarking on the same voyage undertaken by Darwin nearly 200 years previously.

Primarily a landscape artist, Ackroyd frequently depicts rugged and wild settings of the British Isles, capturing them with a subtle and serene beauty that has come to typify his practice. Choosing to look at the region with an artist's eye—in opposition to the scientist's eye of Darwin—he documented his journey in sketchbooks of watercolour drawings. Taking careful illustrative note of the flora and fauna; the geological particularities and rhythm of the landscape; and the delicate interplay of land and water and subsequent play of light that resulted over the islands, Ackroyd created a series of initial works that accurately depicted what

he, and Darwin 200 years before him, had observed on their separate voyages.

The form of Ackroyd's work for the Laboratory —now situated on the south wall of the Gilmour Suite—was of utmost importance to the artist. The final composition needed to illustrate the diverse and complex environment of the Galapagos Islands whilst simultaneously conveying the fascination Ackroyd experienced whilst undertaking his journey there.

Opposite
Norman Ackroyd in his studio with initial prints for *Galapagos* and a scaled model mock up.

Left
Inked plates in Norman Ackroyd's studio for *Galapagos*.

Right
Panel studies for *Galapagos*.

After careful consideration, Ackroyd decided upon a composite form—rather than combining elements of these within one final piece—which would combine 40 stainless steel etchings, each measuring 36 x 72 cm, to create a stainless steel mural measuring 1.44 x 7.2 m in total; interpreted from his portfolio of watercolours. Using the same printing process adopted throughout his practice that gives his work a defining character, Ackroyd engages with the project intensely in the initial stages, then retreats, returning later on with a sense of retrospective to add further detail. First creating a third scale etched maquette, Ackroyd etches and prints the 40 zinc plates, measuring 12 x 24 cm, then repeats this process, painting each scene onto the stainless steel plate and bathing it in acid to transfer the image. The stainless steel plate is then flooded with resin-enriched ink to bring up the relief, with the excess being rubbed away.

This method of printing allows for the effects of light and reflection—a defining feature of Ackroyd's work—to be realised, as the natural light from the Botanic Garden is filtered onto the undercroft in which Ackroyd's work is situated, where it is then reflected across each etching, interacting with the relief to reveal the defining features of the landscape. By depicting these scenes as he had experienced them first hand, Ackroyd attempts to convey the atmosphere of the islands, hopefully passing both his and Darwin's experiences on to the spectator: "The essence of the Galapagos splashed on the wall."

HENSLOW'S WALK
Susanna Heron

Central to Susanna Heron's practice is an interrogation of the relationship between art, architecture and place and how this informs the final outcome of an artwork. Site specificity and the surrounding landscape hold particular resonance in Heron's work, with the idea of 'space' continually explored. The piece created for The Sainsbury Laboratory exemplifies the responsive attitude she assumes throughout her practice, to her surroundings and the project at hand as well as reflecting her personal interest in botany—as seen in previous works such as *Shima: Island and Garden*, a sequence of photographs and prose poem, resulting from her involvement in the regeneration of Eagles Nest garden some 20 years ago. Immersing herself within the Laboratory's work, Heron borrowed digital photographs of 4,951 collations of plant samples from the Cambridge Herbarium to be housed within the Laboratory—these are highly sophisticated visual documents, of native plants collated by John Stevens Henslow, botanist and mentor of Charles Darwin, which explored early ideas on evolution; as a result of conversations with John Parker, then Director to the Botanic Garden, Heron interprets Henslow's work as inspiring Darwin's Theory of Evolution. On developing a fascination for the work of Henslow, Heron's central concern to encourage looking as a means for thought reflects the influence of the botanist and his work upon the aims of the Laboratory today.

Employing her favoured medium of drawings in shallow relief, Heron created four paired drawings along the side-wall to the Laboratory's lecture theatre intricately carved into the yellow French limestone which forms part of the fabric of the building. Heron's initial drawings were formed by taking imprints from both sides of a paint-soaked linen thread, chosen for its tangled grass-like behaviour with Henslow's collations in mind. This apparently random process is no more than a means to an end and the resulting paired drawings appear connected by an invisible presence.

Out of view of the public, the work will only be seen by botanical scientists and employees of the Laboratory—Heron has previously discussed how she likes to make works that will be "happened upon" rather

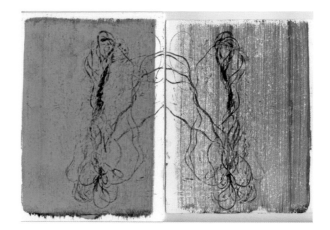

Opposite
Portrait of Susanna Heron in her studio working on models for *Henslow's Walk*.

Above
Sketch for one of the paired images in the stone relief.

than to be expected, making explicit this lack of control by seeking to determine settings for visual events, where variation is inevitable. The location and scale of the wall was highly significant to Heron, in relation to how it affects the space and how this space is experienced by the viewer. Running from one entrance to another, the relief forms an interior connection between two outside spaces, leading to the trees of the Botanic Garden. This narrow corridor is separated from the Lecture Theatre by a glass screen and forms a backdrop to be viewed at a distance from within the Lecture Theatre. As with previous works of Heron's, the relief evokes an organic sense of continuation that guides the narrative of the piece, evolving alongside the form of that onto which it is engraved. Intended to be viewed obliquely and peripatetically from within the corridor, the relief

appears to shift as you walk along its length, encouraging alternative perspectives and a future return to the work, as details, large and small, are revealed.

This piece differs from Heron's usual output of work, however; in that the stone was to be coursed in blocks of stone which were much softer than that which she has worked with previously and therefore would not allow for continuous handling. Heron did not allow a computer programmer scale up her drawings but redrew her initial sketches as digital line drawings at full size and made scale models at real depth to work out the levels of relief. These drawings were then converted to enable the stone to be cut to her original lines by computerised cutting. The joints between the stones form a random grid traversed by the lines of relief and were meticulously pointed to maintain the levels.

Heron builds a poetic narrative that allows a space to be explored depending on the subjective engagement of the observer. Within her work for The Sainsbury Laboratory, the effect of light falling upon the engraving, casting shadows across its relief is particularly poignant for the artist in its giving the work a sense of depth and its highlighting the reciprocal relationship between the site and the work that Heron chooses to explore within her wider practice.

Above
Detail of the stone relief viewed from the Lecture Theatre.

Opposite and overleaf
Details of the stone relief.

HENSLOW'S WALK / SUSANNA HERON **167**

STARBURST
William Pye

Differing from the other artists producing work for The Sainsbury Laboratory, in that he was approached to produce a number of sculptures belonging to an already established series of work; William Pye's general practice does, however, present an incredibly fitting body of work for the aims of Stanton Williams and The Sainsbury Laboratory, in that it interprets and mirrors the natural world—reflected in the flow of water and the subtle rhythms created by form—acting as an accent to the Laboratory itself and the Botanic Garden.

Made from mirror-polished stainless steel, Pye's *Starburst*'s work by jetting water from a lit tube upwards, onto a circular dish of toughened glass, where droplets then burst and radiate, changing and transmuting as they travel to the outer limits of the surface; where gravity then takes hold, as they proceed to drop away. Whilst the four *Starbursts* are part of a larger series of

Opposite
William Pye working on the installation of *Starburst* at The Sainsbury Laboratory.

Above
The *Starburst* sculpture installed at The Sainsbury Laboratory.

work, unrelated to The Sainsbury Laboratory, they have, however, been developed very much in mind of the project at hand. Describing them as "site-specific", Pye's designs for the works were made with the architecture of the building and the landscape of the Garden close at mind. The layout of the trees within the Garden was of particular importance to the design process, with Pye imagining the Starbursts as almost 'interwoven' with the trees.

Light is, again, of utmost importance to Pye, from the effects of the artificial LED lighting—particular to The Sainsbury Laboratory *Starburst*'s—which have been programmed to change colour; in opposition to the effects of the natural light of the Botanic Garden, reflecting off of the mirror polished stainless steel. These works are often highly polished, in order to best capture the qualities of light and reflection created when water moves over their surface. The way in which light has been used can also be considered as site-specific, with Pye developing the sculptures specifically for the project, so that a smooth clear jet of water is created through which light can pass, rather than a "violent splash of water" which has tended to obliterate the light in previous projects. Proving successful, a dramatic ring of light was created in the middle of each *Starburst* with a smoother and more regular pattern of droplets radiating from their centre.

Pye's abstract sculptural work explore issues of form and space through minimalist materials such as stone and steel, whilst simultaneously, and most notably, exploring the possibilities of kinetic materials, in particular, water.

The idea of "contained water" is central to his creation of the Starburst's, viewing this containment as affording him the opportunity to develop sculptures that capitalise upon the effects of water, in a way that is "more dramatic, exciting and animated", which, to Pye, is perfectly suited to the outdoors setting of the Botanic Garden, in which the four sculptures are found.

Above
Light sequencing of the *Starbust* sculpture in situ at The Sainsbury Laboratory.

Opposite
The *Starburst* sculpture at dusk.

Overleaf
Detail of a *Starburst* showing the exploding light and water shaft inside the sculpture; view of The Sainsbury Laboratory from within the trees of the Botanic Garden.

BIOGRAPHIES

STEPHEN DAY

Stephen Day has had a lifelong interest in plants and plant biology. He studied Botany at Cambridge and after graduating took a number of short term jobs, including as a gardener, a garden centre worker and a research assistant at the Plant Breeding Institute, then in Trumpington. Throughout this period he was writing science news stories as a freelance journalist and, shortly before the birth of his first child, he turned to science writing full time. He writes both popular and educational pieces.

Currently based near Ely, Day is completing the second edition of an undergraduate textbook on plant developmental biology, of which he is co-author.

JOHN PARKER

John Parker studied botany at Oxford University, and stayed on for his doctorate to study plant chromosomes and their influence on recombination.

He then moved to London and spent 23 years at Queen Mary College, where he taught genetics and carried out research on the chromosomes, genetics and evolution of plant populations. He was appointed Professor of Botany and Head of Department at the University of Reading in 1992 and after four years took up the post of Director of the Botanic Garden at Cambridge University. In Cambridge, he held academic posts as Professor of Plant Cytogenetics and Curator of the University Herbarium, both in the Department of Plant Sciences. He retired at the end of 2010, having been involved as University representative throughout the whole construction of the Sainsbury Laboratory. At Cambridge, his interests shifted from the mechanisms of evolution to the origins of modern evolutionary thinking. In particular, he has studied the research programme of Professor John Henslow, founder of the University Botanic Garden and mentor of Charles Darwin. In addition to his University appointments, John Parker has been a Trustee of Royal Botanic Gardens Kew, on the Council of the Royal Horticultural Society, an Honorary Research Fellow of the Natural History Museum, a Trustee of the National Fruit Collection, and a Director of the National Institute for Agricultural Botany.

STEVE ROSE

Steve Rose writes on architecture, cinema and other arts. He has been a weekly contributor to *The Guardian* newspaper and website since 1999, operating as a critic, blogger and feature writer on architecture, design and film. He has also written for other newspapers, magazines and websites including *The Independent, The Times, Wallpaper*, Metropolis* and *Uncut*. He is the author of *Eye: The Story Behind The London Eye*, and has contributed to numerous other architecture and cinema books. He lives in London.

INDEX

CREDITS

FUNDER
—*The Gatsby Charitable Foundation*
David Sainsbury, Susie Sainsbury, Peter Hesketh,
Jessica Roberts

CLIENT AND PROJECT OFFICER
—*University of Cambridge*
Michael Bienias, Gordon Millar

STRATEGIC PROJECT MANAGER AND FUNDER'S REPRESENTATIVE
—*Stuart A Johnson Consulting Ltd*
Stuart Johnson

PROJECT ADVISERS
Roger Freedman, Robert McGhee

THE SAINSBURY LABORATORY, UNIVERSITY OF CAMBRIDGE
Elliot Meyerowitz, Ottoline Leyser

PROJECT AND CONTRACT ADMINISTRATOR
—*Hannah - Reed*
Henry Martin, Margaret Winchcomb, Mark Hall, Doug
Howlett, Emel Kus, Michal Wodynski

REPRESENTATIVE USER (LABORATORY)
—*The Gatsby Charitable Foundation*
Alan Cavill

REPRESENTATIVE USER (BOTANIC GARDEN)
—*Cambridge University Botanic Garden*
John Parker, Tim Upson

MAIN CONTRACTOR
—*Kier Regional*
John Henke, Louisa Finlay, Nick Mann, Carl Ayres,
David Baker, Sally Bowles, Matt Bott, George Campbell,
Robert Campbell, Mark Causey, Antony Clark, Libby
Clark, John Coleman, Iain Cox, Richard Crompton,
Nick Davis, Darren Ferry, Keith Ferry, Justin Fletcher,
Paul Geddis, James Griffiths, Sharen Hughes, Ross James,
Abouzar Jahanshahi, Bill Johnson, Ganesh Jothirajan,
Jai Wen Lee, Andy Luck, Marvin Manyepa, Steve
Musson, Guy Osbourne, Alistair Ringer, Ian Squire, Lynn
Summerfield, Tim Swingler

ARCHITECT
—*Stanton Williams*
Ram Ahranov, Andre Baugh, Francesca Bergamini,
Simon Blunden, Stuart Bourne, Alex Buckland, Gioia
Castiglioni, Alistair Cook, Bertil Donker, Tom Finch,
Andy Garton, Elena Gaydar, Sanjay Ghodke, John
Hatton, Gavin Henderson, Kalpesh Intwala, Larissa
Johnston, Nina Langner, Nick Mills, Peter Murray,
Venetia Playne, Patrick Richard, Alan Stanton, Caryl
Stephen, Vera Tang, Michele Tarroni, Moritz Thierfelder,
Hayley Thompson, Paula Trinade, Paul Williams, Henry
Williams, Carmen Yip

STRUCTURAL AND CIVIL ENGINEERS
—*Adams Kara Taylor*
Albert Williamson-Taylor, Steve Toon, Rachel Cleary,
Carlo Diaco, Michael Duff, Katy Eyre-Maunsell, Danny
Hambling, Paul Hutter, Baktasch Spartak, Bhaven Tailor,
Lee Wingate

BUILDING SERVICES ENGINEER
—Arup
Guy Channer, Jennifer DiMambro, Nick Adams, Kelly Adighije, Bibi Banjo, Ian Braithwaite, Alexis Brown, Anna Burbidge, Robert Carmichael, Jac Cross, Mike Ebsworth, Guy Edwards, Tom Fernando, Clare Fisher, Andy Freezer, Anne Gilpin, Adam Martin, Iain Moore, Will Sainsbury, Eddie Scuffell, Nick Simpson, Jodh Singh, Paul Vickers, Julie Wainwright, Morwenna Wilson

COST CONSULTANT
—Gardiner and Theobald
Martin Cash, Stuart Goodchild, Andrew Browne, Kevin Carvill, Mark Dobson, Garry Ford, Ed Wickens

LANDSCAPE ARCHITECT
—Bradley-Hole Schoenaich Landscape Architects
Christopher Bradley-Hole, Brita von Schoenaich

CDM COORDINATOR
—Hannah-Reed
Graham Fowler, Erin Jane Davies

BREEAM ASSESSOR
—Buro Happold Ltd
Simon Wright

ARBORICULTURALIST
—Forbes-Laird Arboricultural Consultancy Ltd
Julian Forbes-Laird

FIRE CONSULTANT
—Arup Fire
David Stow, Gordon Wills

FACADE CONSULTANT
—Arup Facade Engineering
Giorgio Buffoni, Matt Williams, Jonathan Wilson

LIGHTING CONSULTANT
—Arup Lighting
Arfon Davies, Melissa Mak, Kevin Womack

ACOUSTIC CONSULTANT
—Arup Acoustics
Ben Cox, Azu Hatch, Raf Orlowski, Adrian Passmore, Malcolm Wright

BUILDING CONTROL
—Cambridge City Council
Ian Boulton

TRAFFIC CONSULTANTS
—Hannah - Reed
James Martin, Colin Young, Frank Young, Haider Ali

COMMISSIONING AUDIT MANAGER
—Phil Harvey Commissioning Ltd
Phil Harvey

CLERK OF WORKS (M&E)
—Maslin Building Services Limited
Malcolm Maslin

ARTS CONSULTANTS
—InSite Arts Ltd
Sam Wilkinson, Sarah Collicott

FURNITURE CONSULTANT & CONTRACTOR
—Luke Hughes and Company
Luke Hughes

ARTIST
—Galapagos
Norman Ackroyd, Mark Cassey (Photofabrication Ltd.), Niamh Clancy, Jason Hicklin

ARTIST
—Henslow's Walk
Susanna Heron, Mary Hogben (Hogben and Hale Architects), Barry Woodley (Stone Circle), David Ward (lighting advisor)

ARTIST
—*Starburst*
William Pye, Barry Goillau (Benson Sedgewick Engineering), Andrew Hewitt (Artful Logistics), James Larsson (Electronics)

CAMBRIDGE UNIVERSITY BOTANIC GARDEN
—*University of Cambridge*
Rachel Agnew, Paul Aston, Pete Atkinson, Ian Barker, Robert Brett, Heloise Brooke, Pauline Bryant, Alistair Cochrane, Mark Crouch, Juliet Day, Martine Gregory-Jones, Dianne Harrison, Adrian Holmes, John Kapor, Pete Kerley, Alan Langley, Pete Michna, Sally Petitt, Helen Seal, Pat Smith, Brigid Stacey, Phil Starling, Karen Van Oostrum, Simon Wallis, Laura Welford

CLIENT PLANNING AND RESOURCES
—*University of Cambridge*
Tony Minson

CLIENT TEAM
—*University of Cambridge*
David Baulcombe
John Gray

CLIENT ESTATE MANAGEMENT TEAM
—*University of Cambridge*
John Clark, Ravinder Dhillon, Martin Dowling, Phil Hopper, Chris Lawrence, Chris Lewis, Alexis Park, Emma Putterill, Colin Saunders, Rob Simpson, Andrew Snushall, Gerry Walker

CLIENT FINANCE
—*University of Cambridge*
Bernadette McClellan, Gail Russell (Lynxvale), Kerry Sykes

KIER REGIONAL SUBCONTRACTORS
—*Specialist Contractors/ M & E Services*
Balfour Beatty (BBES)

—*Raised Access Flooring*
Bathgate Flooring

—*Screeding - Resin*
Bolidt Synthetic Systems

—*Building B Glasshouse*
Bridge Greenhouses Ltd

—*Shutters, Smoke Ventilation Doors & Flush Metal Doors*
Briton Shutters & Grilles

—*Mastic Jointing*
Construction Sealants

—*Plant Growth*
Conviron

—*Steel Fabrication & Erection*
DGT Structures Ltd

—*Glazed Façade*
Feldhaus

—*Flat Roofing*
Fenland

—*Fire Protection*
Harrison Contracts

—*Air/Thermal Testing*
HRS Services

—*Piling*
Keller Ltd

—*Curtains and Blinds*
Levolux

—*Laboratory Benching*
Luntri

—*Ceramic Tiling*
Neofloors Ltd

—*Poly Tunnel & Shade Hall*
NP Structures

—*Internal Glazing*
Optima

—*Lifts*
Otis

—*Ladders/Handrails/Metalwork*
PAD Contracts

—*Louvres*
PAR Louvres Systems Ltd.

—*Lift Installation*
Phoenix Lifting Systems Ltd

—*Final Clean*
Premier Cleaning Services Ltd

—*Brick/Blockwork*
Proctor Construction Ltd

—*Auditorium Seating*
RACE Furniture

—*Fixtures/Furnishings*
Rackline Limited

—*Groundworks & External*
S & M Contractors

—*Drylining Ceilings*
SCL Interiors

—*Catering Equipment*
Shine Food Machinery

—*Joinery & Ironmongery*
Swift Southern

—*Natural Stone*
Szerelmey

—*Painting and Decorating*
Talbot Decorators

—*Temporary Electrics*
TJ Electrical

—*Precast Concrete Structures*
Trent Concrete Cladding Ltd

—*Screeding Isocrete*
Tyndale Flooring

—*RC and Steel*
Whelan & Grant

—*Soft Landscaping*
Willerby Landscapes Ltd

IMAGE CREDITS

© 2011 Black Dog Publishing Limited,
the authors, architects, artists and photographers.
All rights reserved.

Black Dog Publishing Limited
10A Acton Street
London
WC1X 9NG

T. +44 (0)207 713 5097
F. +44 (0)207 713 8682
E. info@blackdogonline.com
W. blackdogonline.com

All opinions expressed within this publication are those of the authors,
architects and artists and not necessarily of the publisher.

British Library Cataloguing-in-Publication Data.
A CIP record for this book is available from the British Library.

ISBN 978 1 907317 45 3

Black Dog Publishing is an environmentally responsible company.
The Sainsbury Laboratory is printed on FSC accredited paper.

The Sainsbury Laboratory: Science, Architecture, Art DVD contains film and
interview footage further elaborating on aspects of The Sainsbury Laboratory
and Cambridge University Botanic Garden.

architecture art design
fashion history photography
theory and things

**black dog
publishing**

www.blackdogonline.com   london uk